Table of Contents

Introduction

Your Book's Journey: A Travel Guide

By using this book as your guide, you will learn about the publishing industry as a whole, how to think like a publisher, and what steps to take to create a successful book. You will also learn the tools needed to stay on top of current publishing trends and avoid costly mistakes.

It is every writer's dream to see his or her book in the front window of the local bookstore. It is fun to imagine tall, colorful stacks of your books surrounded by throngs of curious readers flipping through the pages while others rush to the cash register with their copy.

In order to make that dream come true, you have to stop thinking like a writer and start thinking like a publisher. For publishers, the dream location is not the bookstore shelf; that shelf is simply a short stop on the way to the real destination . . . a reader's bookshelf. The only bookshelf that truly counts is that of the consumer. Many books and articles guide a writer to an agent, a publisher, or a Print-on Demand printer.

But this book has been written to guide your book into (and then out of) the hands of people who actually paid money to read it.

If you're truly serious about publishing your book, then you need to shake off the fantasy and take a good, hard look at the challenge ahead. This isn't meant to discourage you. On the contrary, the better prepared you are, the more successful you will be in reaching your goals.

The path a writer's work takes through the publishing process, into the retail market, and then onto a consumer's bedside table is arduous. On this journey, you will encounter misleading signposts, publishing experts who just want your money, many paths damaged by overuse, and paths hard to traverse from underuse. But you will also experience a number of wondrous sights and resting places. The sweeps and turns of the path to a published book can be fascinating—but even more profitable and rewarding if you know the lay of the land ahead of time.

As a writer on the verge of publishing, you are enthusiastic about your work and determined to see it through to book form. While these are certainly helpful qualities in battling the challenges ahead, there is one tool to help you overcome the obstacles and push forward during the final stretch: That one key tool is knowledge.

That's where we come in.

By using this book as your guide, you will learn about the industry as a whole, how to think like a publisher, and what steps to take to create a successful book. Step by step, we'll maneuver the book industry together, traveling through publishing, manufacturing, research, and sales on our way to a reader's hands.

The best way to start a journey is to learn as much about your destination as possible. Once you know where you're going, you'll be able to plan your route to get there. So set your writing aside for the moment as we explore the book industry and that oh-so-important destination: the reader.

Chapter One

Today's Book Industry

Many published authors got their deals after proving that their books could sell. They did this by publishing and selling their books themselves. Mark Twain was actually quite famous for having to print and sell his own books because no one else would.

What are some of the questions we have to ask if we are going to join ranks with Mark Twain? *What kinds of people buy books? What kinds of books do they buy? From where do these people buy the books?*

The answers to these questions are changing rapidly. It used to be that if you had a specific need (a job interview, wedding, new baby, etc.) you would go to the store and pick up a book on that topic to educate yourself on the newest thoughts on that subject. Books were the preferred tool for disseminating new information. Not anymore.

Magazines (also a changing animal) hit the scene and trained readers to grab for the "highlights" on a topic. No longer did people feel that they needed a deep, thorough understanding of their topics. They learned that they could "get the gist" in three to five pages at most and, in most cases, do just fine.

Then came the Internet. Think you have lupus? Log on! Want to cultivate a pink-and-white-only garden that your local deer won't eat? Just type in the URL and www .girlydeerresistantgardens.com to the rescue! The people who think they are too busy to read a whole book and cannot find the time to catch up on the stack of magazines piling up on the counter can now have seventy-five words on any given subject electronically handed to their inbox to be downloaded and absorbed in seconds.

But what about novels? Yes, there is still a strong market for beautifully written, well-edited, sharply crafted fiction. Keep in mind, however, that the competition from popular, established authors and celebrities with clever marketing, ghostwriting, and PR teams have driven the chances of a new writer's work appearing on a national chain's bookstore shelves way, way, way down. Therefore, many talented writers are moving to Web-based and print-on-demand digests.

Fans of savvy, edgy writing are flocking to websites to get their daily dose of prose. Every day, established, talented book authors are writing 3,000–5,000 words for readers who will never see those words in a book. 'Zines, Web digests, salons, and blogs have forever changed how fiction readers get their fix.

Even so, there are still a great many first-time authors courted and guided by established publishers, and even as this is being written, there is a freshman novel being purchased for $1.2 million somewhere. I hate to have to tell you this, but . . . that won't be you. I can confidently say that because such deals only happen once in a great while, and the rate is slowing because editors must report their decisions to committees of accountants. (If you are one of the eleven people to whom this sort of deal has happened, just get in touch with me and I will happily transfer the cost of this book into your already bulging bank account.)

Quite a few freshmen authors got their deals because of their contacts or their family's contacts. (Sorry, it's true. . . .) Other authors with their first book deals have such a large and profitable online following that publishers are clamoring to work with them. (Do YOU have more than a million followers?)

Then there is the already famous. At one point in 2014, seventeen of the top twenty non-fiction books were written by Reality TV stars.

But many published authors got their deals after proving that their books could sell. They did this by publishing and selling their books themselves. Self-publishing has become a very popular way for authors to invest in their book's future success.

If you have the means and focus, publishing your own book can often give it a better chance of being picked up by a traditional publisher. It can also be a terrific way to skip the tradition publishing route altogether and become a successful (and more profitable) author on your own.

Forget the naysayers who insist books are not the way of the future. The future is filled with those who will always be seeking connection, inspiration, and information.

Simply put, books are not dead. In spite of the Cassandra-like warnings from experts over the last 100 years that the book is becoming obsolete, books are here to stay. Newspapers, radio, and television did not kill the book, nor will the Internet, Netflix, or iPod do so. Books offer a sense of comfort and reliability that other mediums simply can't touch.

For people who hear a particularly compelling speaker and want to learn more about his or her message, there are books. For those riding to work each day who want to escape into a good story, there are books. For those who want to deeply explore a topic and have a reference to which they can always go to, there are books.

Let's return to our previous questions: Why do people buy books? What kinds of people buy books? What kinds of books do they buy?

People buy books for entertainment and information. Many book readers express a sense of connection and community that cannot be duplicated by videos. Books bought today are inspirational, informational, entertaining.

No matter what form or format it might take, there are readers who will be in the market for your book.

Let's look at the path a book takes from publisher to store to reader. To do this, we will have to agree upon current definitions for some industry terms. These may or may not be the same definitions of similar terms in other industries, but you're living in the publishing world now, so it's best you learn the lingo. Your first vocabulary lesson begins with the three places most stores go to get their books: publishers, distributors, and wholesalers.

PUBLISHERS

Publishers are the manufacturers of books. They usually own the rights to the material and pay for the developing, design, and printing of the book. They will edit, copy edit, proofread, design, lay out, and print the book. They will sell a book to a store at a discount of the retail price. That discount is usually between 40 and 48 percent. It can sometimes be 50 percent or more if the store is part of a co-op or chain that has a central warehouse or agrees to pay for the shipping costs of the books.

The store or the buyer for the group of stores will contact the publisher, place a purchase order for books, and expect to receive them in five to seven days. They expect to be billed for these books, but will usually require at least ninety days to pay.

If you want to become a publisher, here are a few things you should think about. You have to plan and budget carefully. Small presses usually aren't paid for three to four months. It's just the way things are. Plan for it now.

Now, are you ready for the big hit? Publishers may not even see that money because the books are bought returnable. Fully returnable. One hundred percent. No backsies.

After a publisher has shipped a book to a store, the bookstore has the right to ship it right back for any reason.

Please make sure that you factor returns (the shipping costs, processing costs) into your profit and loss plans. When deciding on a budget for your self-published book, figure bookstore returns at 40 percent. This is much higher than the industry average, but statistics show that self-published books have a much harder time getting into bookstores and a much harder time selling through the registers than traditionally published books.

The reasons for this are many. Bookstores are often reluctant to risk their limited dollars and shelf space on an unproven publishing company's first book. You can get around this, but without an established, experienced publishing company's PR and marketing efforts behind your book, you may experience lower sell-through than the industry average of 70 percent.

There are very successful small presses that claim very few returns. We interviewed a number of publishers with return percentages in the low teens and here is what they suggest:

- Avoid black or dark covers when possible. Black covers accentuate scuffing and smudge marks more than other colors, thus increasing the odds of returns.
- Print extra dust jackets (20 percent over) for hardcover books. In most cases, a dust jacket replacement will make a "damaged" book look as good as new.

Any excess jackets may be used for promotional purposes.

- When using a POD printer, make the book returnable/destroy. That way, bookstores will have less costs involved in returns and will be more willing to reorder your books if they sell.

- Avoid spiral binding when possible. This type of binding tends to get damaged in transit, as well as damaging the covers of other books in the same package. Also, if the name is not visible on the spine, the book may not sell very well!

- Pre-price your books with Bookland/EAN barcodes. By barcoding your book, you will avoid retailers' stickers and smudge marks from sticker removal. Some (most) bookstores require a pre-specific barcode because stores do not have the time or interest in stickering books.

- Notify wholesalers and major book retailers at least three months before new editions are available, so automatic computer reorder triggers can be turned off for higher-sell-through and fewer returns of old books.

- Promote, promote, promote!

- Create a "stay in place" program where you offer stores an additional 90 days to pay if they keep your books on the shelf.

Publishers have also developed strategies for dealing with books returned in shelf-worn condition. This is usually the case, since by the time the publisher receives them back, they have been handled five to seven times in the marketplace (printer to publisher to wholesaler to retailer to returns center to wholesaler to publisher). Some options for using returned books are:

- Send to media contacts when arranging promotional events
- Use for contests and give-away promotions
- Mark down and sell to discount buyers, remainder houses, book fairs or swap meets
- Sell to your friends, family, and employees at a discount
- Strip and rebind damaged books with fresh covers.
- Donate to charitable organizations

DISTRIBUTORS

Bookstores also get books from distributors. A distributor handles all of the après-production elements of getting a book onto a store's shelves. The good ones go a step further and help you get a book onto a reader's bedside table. Publishers agree to funnel all of their sales, warehousing, shipping, and billing through the distributor. They do this work for a percentage of the billing generated by the sale of the publisher's books.

Like publishers, distributors sell a book to a bookstore at a discount of the retail price. That discount is usually between 45 and 50 percent. Bookstores that order books from a distributor expect to receive the books in five to seven days.

So, if bookstores get about the same terms and about the same schedule, why do they go to a distributor instead of directly to the publisher? Some bookstores (especially bookstore chains) are not interested in setting up new, small, or regional publishers in their ordering and accounting systems for just a few books. They rightly weigh the benefits of a publisher's book against the time and trouble necessary to order it, and if the balance does not come out in the book's favor, they skip it. How do new and small publishers avoid this terrible fate? They sign exclusive agreements with a distributor.

But not all distributors are created equal. There are good and not-so-good distributors.

Be careful when choosing a distributor. Make sure you do your research.

The good ones will keep the books in their warehouses, send their reps out to bookstores to present the books to the buyers, take orders, ship the books, negotiate the cost, bill the stores, and after taking their cut, hand over all the profits paid back to the publisher. When possible, the reps who sold the books to the book buyers will give the publisher feedback as to the reaction the books received. Direct, front-line, market-driven feedback is the key to a good distributor. They can help you keep your determination and focus when books are taking a long time to sell. More often, the feedback can teach a publisher about the changes necessary for the next print run of the book to increase the salability.

The not-so-good distributors will warehouse a publisher's books and wait for a bookstore to order them. Once the order comes in, they will ship, bill, and handle the accounting, but there will be no follow-up, no creativity, or marketplace-driven marketing or feedback.

Contact a few of the publishers listed on the distributor's website and ask how they like working with their distributor. Call your local independent bookstore and ask if they ever see a rep that carries that particular distributor.

WHOLESALERS

Huh? Didn't we just cover them? Nope! In the book world, wholesalers are a whole other animal.

For our purposes, wholesalers are companies that buy your books at a deep discount and hold them in their warehouses so that Internet and "brick and mortar" stores can order the books from them. Bookstores like to use wholesalers for a number of reasons, namely: speed, convenience, and less financial exposure.

When a bookstore orders a book from a wholesaler, they will usually get their order in twenty-four hours. Next-day service is the standard from the top wholesalers. The discount a store can usually expect to receive off the retail price of the book from a wholesaler is 40 to 45 percent. What the bookstore loses in profit margin, they often make up in convenience and risk aversion. A book ordered from a wholesaler can be combined and shipped with hundreds of other books.

Some stores hire wholesalers to stock, manage, and handle all aspects of their book departments. There are large "big-box" chains that happily hand their title selection and discount negotiations over to a wholesaler that will manage the entire department for them. The same can sometimes be true for libraries. There are many U.S. library systems dependent upon wholesalers for all their new books. People at the chain or library office work with the wholesalers and oversee the choices, but how closely that is managed depends upon each individual situation.

If you want your book to have a chance at a bookstore chain like Barnes & Noble or Books-A-Million, and if you don't want to use a distributor, a wholesaler is your next best bet.

The two biggest book wholesalers for the book industry right now are Ingram and Baker & Taylor. You can find their application process for new publishers on their websites. The links are listed on the CD in your Write 2 Print software package and at the end of this book. Send your books in with the proper paperwork and try to get your titles into at least one of these wholesaler's warehouses.

If you are accepted, you will be selling your books to the wholesaler at a discount of at least 55 percent. They will usually order only as many as they need to fulfill the demand coming in from their customers . . . stores and libraries. If they are overstocked or books come back from the stores, they will return those books to you for a full refund. (Having fun yet?)

While daunting, using a wholesaler is also a good idea if there is a growing demand for your book from online bookstores such as Amazon.com. We will cover how Amazon.com works and how to work with them in a later chapter, but keep in mind that using a wholesaler is a great way to get "in" with the big-name stores and online retailers.

Only you can judge your situation, but now you have a good foundation of knowledge to help you plan your way onto the shelves of a store near you.

POD (PRINT ON DEMAND)

Now . . . The REALLY good news!

Several years ago, Ingram Book came up with a program to allow publishers to print low-demand books one at a time using digital printing. Amazon soon purchased a digital printing company as well and these two companies (Ingram and Amazon) launched onto a new business model that would change publishing as we know it.

Let's take a look at PRINT ON DEMAND (POD).

POD is NOT a type of printing. POD is a business model that uses digital printing to print just as many books as are needed at a time. In the past, publishers would print several thousand books in anticipation of sales and pray that they were correct. Often the printed books were not able to keep up with demand, leading to shortages and unhappy readers. MORE often, the printed books sat in a warehouse for years before being pulped or sold for pennies on the dollar.

Digital printing now makes it possible to print 1 or 100 books at a time in a manner that still allows a publisher to make a (smaller) profit and minimize all the financial risk.

How does this help you? As a small press or first-time author, you can use POD service providers to make your book available to Amazon.com customers, bookstores, libraries and your own website for a FRACTION of what it would cost 20 years ago.

"But what about the quality?" asks the smart small press publisher.

It is terrific. Now.

A few years ago, the quality of digital printers was far below the quality of off-set printers for a number of reasons. The printers purchased and used by the two biggest POD service providers (Ingram—Lightning Source and Amazon—CreateSpace) were old and inconsistent. The paper bought in bulk by these two companies was far inferior to the nicer, heavier paper purchased by offset printers.

In the last few years, these two giants (Lightning Source and CreateSpace) have upgraded their digital printing equipment and the paper options, cover options and even the glue used has all been improved to meet or, at times, exceed the materials used at off-set printing houses.

So, how does it work?

Ingram now offers small presses a service called INGRAMSPARK (formerly Lightning Source). Amazon still offers small presses a number of services under the umbrella of CREATESPACE.

You sign up for each service and give them your publisher imprint name, your personal and tax information and your bank information. This allows the company to deposit any money you make into your account and send you detailed reports for your tax and financial records.

Each time someone orders your book, they will print the copy ordered and ship it out to the customer on your behalf. They will deduct the printing costs from what is owed you and deposit the rest into your bank account. In the upcoming chapters, we will go over the set up process, the exact dollars and profits to be expected, and the reasons to use each company.

But before we leave off of POD, we need to explain the biggest benefit of using them.

If bookstores, airport stores, libraries, and other brick and mortar retailers are part of your sales goals, you HAVE to be in the major wholesalers.

These wholesalers do not have the space or interest in holding your books for you while you go after the retailers. It would cost them too much money to do this for the millions of authors and small presses that publish every year.

POD is the best and (in many cases) only way into Ingram, Baker & Taylor, America West and other wholesalers.

IngramSpark has agreements with Ingram and many other wholesalers that allow you to get your book listed with them so that orders can be fulfilled.

To repeat. IngramSpark is the best and in many cases, only way into the retailers.

Nicole Riley from New Shelves Books has offered these ideas when researching distributors.

Some Questions to ask a Prospective Distributor:

▶ How long have you been in the distribution business?

▶ How many publishers/companies do you distribute?

▶ How many titles/products do you distribute?

▶ What genres/categories do you distribute?

▶ How many sales reps does your company have? (In-house or commission only.)

▶ What are your set-up/cataloging fees if you were to accept me as a client?

▶ What percentage of net sales do you take as your distribution fee?

▶ Are there any additional monthly charges that I might incur? (Warehousing, order fulfillment, returns processing, administration, etc.)

▶ How far in advance of my release date do you need to properly sell my title?

▶ What is the length of your agreement?

What you should expect from a distributor:

▶ To correctly list your title data for ordering with all the major brick and mortar, online retailers, and wholesalers.

- ▶ A thorough presentation of your title to the major retailers and wholesalers in their territory.
- ▶ Willingness to work around your schedule and not be a slave to their own production and sale schedule.
- ▶ Availability for inclusion of your title in the tradeshows at which the distributor exhibits/attends.
- ▶ Timely processing of your title's orders and returns.
- ▶ Monthly printed or online sales and inventory reports.
- ▶ Monthly communication via phone or e-mail to discuss progress.
- ▶ Access to marketing and advertising opportunities with wholesalers, retailers, and/or consumers.
- ▶ Continual sales of your title even after the first season.

What you should not expect from a distributor:

- ▶ Miracles! Your books will not magically appear on every bookstore shelf.
- ▶ To do all the work. Without a solid, well-planned advertising and marketing campaign geared toward your audience, the distributor will not be able to sell your title to the retailers and wholesalers. This is the publisher/author's responsibility and not the distributor.
- ▶ Guaranteed sell through. Once a distributor gets your books onto a bookshelf, it is the publisher's job to make sure that they fly off the bookstore shelf.

Getting into a distributor's catalog is a difficult task. It is a very competitive segment, and good distributors are careful to only take on clients whom they feel will be successful. Every successful publisher increases a distributor's reputation; an unsuccessful publisher can drive a distributor's reputation down.

Here is a list of things you can do when approaching distributors to improve your chances:

- Have your book/advanced reader copy professionally designed. Presentation is key to all products including books, so a professional design is a must.
- Have your book professionally edited. Do not use your cousin Susie who's an English teacher at your local high school as your editor. You need a professional to help you make your book the best it can be from a content standpoint.
- Have a detailed plan for your marketing, advertising, and PR. Also, include your budget of what you intend to spend. We see so many submissions from publishers/authors who do not have a plan to let consumers or their target audience know the books exists.
- Be willing to listen to the professional. Distributors, retailers, publicists and book shepherds make their living selling books. If they give you advice regarding your book, take it. It may mean the difference in selling a ton or none.

Without a solid, well-planned advertising/marketing campaign geared toward your audience, the distributor will not be able to sell your title to the retailers and wholesalers.

Distribution contracts usually start at two-year terms. They are taking a big risk by taking you on, and they want to safeguard that decision by protecting their investment with a minimum two-year term. It takes at least two years to launch a program properly and to start to see results. They are well within their rights to ask this of a publisher. However, you are well within your rights to get certain agreements from them as well. You should be able to get out of your contract if you can show that your books did not receive the activities contracted.

Now, some very good distributors offer warehousing and billing only, for a lower cost. Some publishers wish to handle their own sales and marketing, and just have someone handle the warehousing, fulfillment, and billing side of the business. This segment of distribution is usually called a fulfillment contract.

A distributor's cut could vary from 25 to 40 percent of the net billing of each book. Fulfillment contracts are usually 10 to 15 percent of the net billing. Just about every distributor has additional monthly fees, and most require an initial deposit for new clients. This applies to fulfillment contracts as well.

Before you balk, keep in mind that it is very difficult, expensive, and time consuming to handle your own warehousing, purchase shipping materials, and learn how to ship exactly how each store wishes their shipments to arrive . . . and everyone is different. (It's a little joke they like to play on publishers. I am convinced that bookstore owners get together every two years to devise slightly altered, yet completely incomprehensible, shipping and trafficking instructions.) Then comes the billing, monthly statements, handling claims for books damaged in transit, taking in returns, and reconciling the amount due with what the bookstore believes is due.

After that, consider the money and time it takes to tell the country's thousands of buyers about your books. The sales reps working for distributors have long-standing relationships with the book buyers in your hometown, across the country, and in the major chains. You would not be able to start a fledgling relationship on your own with these buyers. What an experienced sales rep can often do with a phone call, you could rarely accomplish with six months and a great deal of research, e-mails, flyers, catalogs, paperwork, and free samples.

But nothing replaces a publisher's drive and efforts. The main thing to remember is that a distributor is often as good or as bad as the relationship between the publisher and the distributor. If yours is one of thousands of books on the oppression of clover farmers in New Guinea in your distributor's catalog, you will not get the time and attention you desire. If you are not out there pushing your book into the press and media, creating a demand for your distributor to work with, they will not keep you for long.

Take your time choosing a distributor. Make sure you are a good fit and that you both share the same goals for your books. If you cannot find a good fit with the distributors that are willing to carry your book, consider the fulfillment contract idea and do your own marketing and sales for the first year. Better to wait and do for yourself than be trapped in a loveless "marriage" with the wrong distributor.

If you want your book to have a chance at a bookstore chain like Barnes & Noble or Books-A-Million, and if you don't want to use a distributor, a wholesaler is your next best bet.

Chapter Two

Getting Set up With Wholesalers,
POD and EBooks all on your own!

DECIDED TO PRINT ON DEMAND?
YOU WILL NEED INGRAMSPARK AND CREATESPACE

I have been asked one question more than any other. "Do
I need IngramSpark or Lightning Source if I have Create
Space?" I know it is tempting to avoid the extra expense
and hassle of taking on a second POD provider, but I want
to take a moment and share some of the experiences we've
had here with our POD work to help you answer the question: DO YOU NEED BOTH?

Yes.

CreateSpace does a terrific job with Amazon.

CreateSpace charges less for printing and set up fees
than IngramSpark.

CreateSpace does offer "Extended Distribution" for
bookstores and libraries. (Sort of . . . more later.)

IngramSpark charges set up fees and a lot more for proofs than CreateSpace does.

But . . .

CreateSpace's "Extended Distribution" is only fully available to those books using a CreateSpace ISBN. (You should always buy your own ISBNs and have a direct relationship with your book's brand and ISBNs).

Even if your book has extended distribution and CAN be bought by bookstores, it most likely WON'T. Bookstores do not relish the idea of giving their biggest competitor money.

In addition, the extended distribution offered by CreateSpace is ACTUALLY LSI! CS uses LSI for the distribution. They do not, however, offer competitive discounts to the bookstores, further narrowing your chances of being stocked.

You will be instantly relegated to the pile of "self published" books before the buyer has a chance to review the quality. Lightning Source allows your book the chance to be ordered in many countries and formats that CreateSpace does not.

So . . .

Use CreateSpace for Amazon. They do a great job and take less money for each sale.

Use IngramSpark in ADDITION so that you can be ordered by the bookstores and Libraries from the large wholesalers with which they prefer doing business.

Use your own, Bowker provided, ISBN so that you have the benefits of your publishing company's brand on all databases.

Don't cheap out. IngramSpark and CreateSpace are two different tools for two different markets. If you don't want to be in the retail store and library market, then you don't need Lightning Source. But if stores and libraries are your goal, then spend the money to provide the books to them in the manner that gives them the best chance of saying "yes."

Finally . . .

If you really cannot stand the thought of using more than one POD provider, go with Lightning Source, it will allow you access to more venues even if it makes you less money per unit.

These two links will walk you through the process:

www.ingramspark.com

www.createspace.com

When you go there you will need:

- Name and Address of publishing entity
- ISBN Prefix or Source Code (The first 9 digits of your ISBN number will be this)
- Name of Bank, name on account, routing and account number for checking account
- Amex, Visa, or MasterCard number, expiration date, mailing address and CVC
- Log in and password to be used

- Contact names and info decided upon. (Name, Address, Phone, emails)
- Is your company a sole propriotorship., LLC, corporation, etc.?
- Social Security Number or Employer Identification Number (EIN)

HOW TO DO YOUR OWN EBOOK DISTRIBUTION

Here are some questions that keep authors up nights:

- What is the best way to get my eBook up on all the major platforms?
- How do I get set up?
- What files do I use?
- Do I use Smashwords? BookBaby?
- Do I need to pay someone a cut or a fee to do my eBook distribution?

AAAAAAARRRRRRRRRGGGGGGGHHHH!

Here are the answers:

The best way to get your eBook up on all major platforms is to spend an hour setting up accounts with Kindle, Nook, Kobo, Googlebooks and iTunes. The rest can wait. Seriously. Kindle alone is more than 90 percent of eBook sales; so with Nook, Kobo, Googlebooks and iTunes included, you are ALL SET.

How do I get set up? EASY! Here are the links you need to set up your own accounts:

KINDLE
https://kdp.amazon.com/self-publishing/signin

NOOK
www.NOOKpress.com

KOBO
https://secure.kobobooks.com/auth/Kobo/login

iBOOKS
https://itunesconnect.apple.com/
(make sure you have a MAC for this one . . .
they do not let PCs upload files)

GOOGLEBOOKS
https://books.google.com/partner/add-books-form

The files you will need are: .epub and .prc. Most eBook platforms use .epub, but Kindle needs a .prc (or .mobi) file to look really good.

If you don't know anyone who can turn your word document or pdf into an .epub or .prc file, email me at info@ newshelves.com and I will get you hooked up. DO NOT pay more than $1 a page for this service. Too many authors are paying WAY too much!

You CAN use BookBaby and Smashwords to do your book. They are both great companies, but they take a cut of your sales and very often the look of your eBook is not as professional or as top line as it should be. If you don't mind giving up a percentage of your sales, they are a good option.

For about an hour of your time as an investment, however, you can EASILY set up your own accounts.

HOW TO APPLY TO WHOLESALERS

If your business model shows that POD is not for you and you don't want to hire a distributor, then you will need to get into one of the wholesalers . . . Ingram Book Group has a ten-book minimum policy for new clients. If you have ten books or more, www.ingrambook.com offers new publishers a questionnaire to fill out. Sample books and the provided paperwork should then be sent to Ingram at their LaVergne, Tennessee, office. They will review the books and decide whether to accept your titles into their system. Baker & Taylor does not have the same limits and thresholds.

Baker & Taylor accepts new publishers with their Publisher Partnership program. Contact the Baker & Taylor Publisher Relations Department and request a Publisher Partner Application. By filling out this application and submitting it with a $495 setup fee, you are agreeing to a 55 percent discount and ninety day terms. By signing up with this program, you will soon receive orders from one or more of their four warehouses.

The books stocked at Baker & Taylor OR Ingram will then be available for order by Amazon.com or any bookstore in the country.

WARNING: These two companies take a VERY small percentage of the books presented to them. If you are determined to have your book sold into the wholesalers directly, be prepared to offer a great deal of proof that you will have strong sales to make it worth their while. You will have to be VERY persuasive!

Chapter Three

Find a Publisher or Be a Publisher?

When you are an author, all you have to worry about is who will want to read your book. When you are a self-publisher, you have to worry about who will buy your book.

By now, you have a better idea of the opportunities out there, as well as how your book may fit into the grand scheme of things. There are many decisions you will have to make in the upcoming months. The first, most important decision is whether you want to publish your book or have it published by someone else.

Authoring a book is a time-consuming, exhausting business. Publishing a book is a time-consuming, expensive, risky business. Both choices are ripe with opportunity and possibilities, but demand a very different set of skills and efforts.

As a publisher, your first job is not to write your book; your first job is to identify those potential readers and find out where they keep their wallets. Seriously. I know it is not as soulful and art-laden as writing, but it's actually the all-important first step. If you skip this step in your rush to the page, you will not get to live out the dream of seeing your book in a store window.

So, it is time to ask some hard questions. And as you answer these questions, the biggest question of all is "Are you sure?" See . . . it is easy for us to THINK we know the answers to these questions. As an author, I fall into the trap of THINKING I know the answer and often am tempted to skip the actual research. After all, who knows the small publisher better than I? (Answer: LOTS OF PEOPLE.)

It is not enough to think I know the answer, I need to get out into the market and find hard data with actual proof.

As we go through the questions ahead, please, please, please, please, commit to going online, into your local store and local libraries and getting the REAL answers from the front lines.

Store managers, librarians, clerks and those who work day to day with books and see what readers actually buy know a LOT more than I do. I depend upon them and their experience far more than my own (and I'm BRILLIANT!).

Ready?

WHO WILL WANT TO READ YOUR BOOK?

(Hint: The answer is not "everybody." Very few people, statistically, will want to read your book.) It's necessary to identify your audience. If you are able to write for a specific group of people, you have a greater chance of reaching a larger number of those people.

So, let's break it down:

- How old are they?
- How do they spend their days?
- How much time do they have to read?
- Are you sure?
- What do their lives look like?
- Do they actually buy books?
- Are you sure?
- Where else can they get this information if they really tried? (Magazines, Internet, Podcasts, TV)
- Why is your book a better choice than that other source for them?
- Will THEY think your book is a better choice for them?
- Are you sure?

WHO WILL WANT TO BUY YOUR BOOK?

This is not always the same group as those who want to read your book. Many people may want to read it, but you are in the market to find people who want to BUY your book.

For instance, if you have written an early reader chapter book, your readers will be children. However, the buyer will be librarians and parents. While it is important to write your book for the reader, it is just as important to shape your book for the buyer. (Themes that the parents approve of, covers that look like other books the kids and parents liked.)

If you have written a high-priced sauce cookbook using native Southwestern peppers, you will not be able to sell as many in a poor Philadelphia neighborhood.

To repeat, when you are an author, all you have to worry about is who will want to read your book. When you are self-publisher, you have to worry about who will buy your book. So ask yourself:

- Who has the disposable income to buy a book on this subject?
- Where do they live?
- Are you sure?
- Where do they shop?
- What else are they reading?
- Did they buy those books they are reading or check them out at the library?

HOW WILL THOSE PEOPLE HEAR ABOUT YOUR BOOK?

(Second hint: Not through "word of mouth." Spontaneous word of mouth does not exist. Word of mouth happens through heavily bankrolled samples and MBA-level backroom positioning with months of groundwork.) You know who your potential readers are; how are you going to reach them?

Do they shop in bookstores? Then maybe you should budget for in-store displays and newsletter advertising.

Do they shop online? Investigate the advertising and marketing programs at online retailers. Learn how to optimize your book's pages at Amazon and BN.com and work daily to drive traffic to your book online.

Do they mainly buy books at seminars and through work? Develop a corporate sales and speaking tour plan to reach them. Book an author tour.

Do they read reviews? Start sending out copies to every reviewer online and in print. You will need hundreds of reviews to get even the smallest bit of attention.

Flesh out the answers to these questions fully before you write those first opening lines.

Please be ruthless at this stage of your evaluation before you spend time and money on a book project. Your goal is to think like a publisher now, and you may find that your book project would make a better magazine article or serial podcast program.

Only proceed after ascertaining that there is solid evidence that your idea will work in book form. Remember, many successful writers make their fortune writing outside of the world of books. Magazines, websites, and blogs are valid and honorable mediums and may be the perfect place to share some of your work.

That said, don't lose heart. You are a writer and, therefore, full of ideas. If your first idea for a book project doesn't pass the reader test, then move on to the next. You have a book in you; otherwise, you never would have started this journey in the first place. It's better to learn the hard lessons now so that you can be a bigger success later.

MAKING YOUR BOOK AVAILABLE TO THE READER

So now that we know who your readers are, where will they find your book? A bookstore is the obvious choice—local bookstores, big chain bookstores—but there are many other venues you might want to consider as well.

Books are on sale in big-box superstores, boutiques, online discounters, truck stops, supermarkets, restaurants, book fairs, and anywhere there is a cash register. Books are moving into every retail outlet imaginable, but how do they get there?

You have identified who your readers will be, come up with compelling evidence that those readers will actually want a book on your subject enough to spend money on it, and have a plan on how to get your book in front of those readers. Armed with this knowledge, you are in a good position to make the next big decision: Do you try to find a publisher, or will you become a publisher?

LEAVE IT TO THE PROS

All of the homework you have done will help you get published. Publishers worth their salt will ask you who your target readers are and how you plan to reach them with your message. You will need to convince the publisher that you have done your homework and can prove that your book will sell. The big question is . . . if you have done all the research and removed most of the risk, why would you need a publisher?

Well, for several reasons:

- *You don't want to be a publisher.* If you are like most authors, the joy is in the writing. The numerous, often stressful, decisions that come with publishing books are best left to those who want to be a publisher. If you aren't interested in assuming this role, take comfort with your legion of author brethren. Better to know what you want than to fight against nature.

- *They have more money than you do*—money that can market your book and help turn your beautiful manuscript into a beautiful book. Even beautiful books can fail. Books don't always make back the money spent on creating them. If you suffered heart palpitations with the last sentence, you might be more comfortable letting someone else take the risk.

- *They have the editors, designers, and experience to create a book the bookstores will want.* As you will learn in later chapters, if you want to compete with the other books on the shelves, you will need to recruit skilled individuals to join your cause. Friends and family don't count. If you don't want to take the time to seek out and hire professionals, then it might be better to let a publisher use its resources.

- *They have well-established marketing and sales channels that will flow your book directly into the buyers' hands.* Established publishers have the history and reputation necessary to walk your book into a bookstore without having to justify the decision at the same level you would. Bookstores don't know you; you have no history of success. If a publisher chooses your book, the bookstores, in many cases, trust their judgment.

If you're feeling up to a challenge and are confident in yourself and your book project, then becoming a publisher just might be the best decision you could make.

Still think you're up to the challenge of becoming a publisher? Before you jump to that option, you need to do some soul-searching. Even though the business side of publishing may be a good fit, you need to make sure the emotional side of publishing is as well. Why do you want to become a publisher?

Let's look at some of the wrong reasons to choose to publish your own book:

- *My book is perfect and I don't want to have some publisher change it.* Every professionally published and commercially successful book in existence had an editor. Or six.
- *I want total control of the process.* "I'm just such a perfectionist" is the cry of many self-published authors when asked why they did not go the more traditional route. The fact is, in most cases, the end product they "published" proves that they were rank

amateurs and the only perfect thing about them was their egos.

- *I think I can do as good a job and make more on each book.* Well, that is a tricky one. Yes, you can make more money on each book sold than if you went with a publisher, but you will have a lot of work to do to get to that point. Do you have a plan to move more books than a publisher with Barnes & Noble's president on speed dial? Do you have $10-15K to spend on creating and marketing the book properly? Can you afford to lose that money?

If some of these questions lead you to a decision, then consider the benefits of a publishing deal. You can find a number of publishers that are accepting manuscripts or seek out an agent to assist you in your goal of becoming a published author.

On the other hand, if you're feeling up to a challenge and are confident in yourself and your book project, then becoming a publisher just might be the best decision you could make.

DIY PUBLISHING

If you're still with us, then you already have two important qualities any good publisher possesses: drive and determination. While there are certainly some circumstances in which it may be easier and even a good idea to seek out a publisher, there are also many good reasons to become a publisher. Let's look at a few:

- *You are a professional with a large and growing client base and you need/want a book to attract new clients.* Doctors, financial planners, lawyers, and mental health practitioners are great examples of this.

- *Bookstores are not going to be the only part of your book sales plan.* If you are aware of the fact that almost 75 percent of books in the U.S. are sold online and want to focus exclusively on this market, you don't really NEED most of what traditional publishers offer.

- *You are already a manufacturer or product merchant and a book on a particular subject will dovetail nicely with your current business model.* Can you do a book far more cheaply because you only offer digital or electronic products? Do you already have a channel into the retailers? Then again, you may not need a traditional publisher.

- *You consider this book project as a way to learn the ropes on your way to starting your own publishing company.* (Better to experiment and make mistakes on your own book rather than someone else's.)

- *You want to test the waters regionally to draw enough attention and interest from national publishers that it will increase the deal you can strike on your first traditional publishing agreement.* The higher you start, the higher you can go.

Whatever your reason may be—just make sure it's a good one—you are going to be a published author and, by extension, a publisher. So, what separates a first book by a new publisher from a self-published book? In upcoming chapters, we will discuss using experienced people to help shape your books, but before you proceed, here is a simple checklist of what you will need:

- A mentor with professional publishing experience
- Examples of books you love that sold well
- A professional editor
- An experienced copy editor and proofreader
- A cover designer with a portfolio of book covers and references from other publishers
- A great book designer with book experience
- An eBook designer who knows how to program and design a cutting-edge eBook
- Enough money to pay for all the elements a professionally published book will demand
- The name of your publishing company (which in no way reflects your name or the name of any of your books)
- A website domain reserved for your publishing company and book

MEASURING SUCCESS

Now is a good time to take a break and figure out what "success" means to you. For many first-time authors, success equates with "instant bestseller." If this is your idea of success, you need to re-evaluate. Your book will not be an instant bestseller. Want to know how I can state that so bluntly? There is no such thing as an instant bestseller. Bestselling books are cultivated, cajoled, and financed into becoming bestsellers; they simply do not hit the top of the charts overnight.

So, with the idea that you will have an instant bestseller out, what do you consider success? Success is different for each person. It's a good idea to think about what you must achieve with this book project to be happy with your efforts. For some, holding the finished product in their hands is success enough. Others cannot be content until they have sold a certain number of copies. So, if you are one whose hard work and sense of accomplishment in seeing a project finished is reward enough, then feel free to proceed to the next chapter and begin your next step toward success. For those of you whose success is measured in quantity, read on.

Here are some sobering statistics from Nielsen Bookscan, a company that tracks the sales of more than 6 million books in the United States:

- Each year, only two to five books sell more than a million copies each.

- Less than 1 percent of the books published this year sold more than 500 copies. That's it.
- This year, major TV stars went on daytime talk shows, hawked their wares, showed up on NPR and still sold less than a few thousand books. The vast majority of books published by major publishing houses lose money. Far more books published by small presses lose money. MORE THAN 80 PERCENT% OF BOOKS PUBLISHED LOSE MONEY.

This isn't meant to make you change your mind or discourage you in any way. I just want you to get a grasp on the book industry and realize how unpredictable it can be. Knowledge is power, remember? The more realistic your goals, the better able you will be to achieve those goals. Besides, once you have invested in this project, you are going to be looking for results. If your goals are in line with a realistic idea of success, then you are going to be much happier with yourself and your accomplishments.

Now the big question. What does it take to sell 1,000 copies, 5,000 copies, 100,000 copies?

If you are going to make a real push for your book into the mainstream of the American readership, you will need a plan, the time to work it, a strong will, good timing, a tenacious nature, and a great deal of luck.

Many well-written, marketable books never sell more than a few hundred copies, while a number of "questionable" titles rise far above their publishers' expectations. There is a quality of randomness when a book catches hold of the public's imagination. As much as we in the industry would like to think we have the magic formula worked out, we are as clueless as the rest when a book races to the top of the charts.

There is no proven formula for creating a bestseller, but bestsellers do share some foundational elements. In upcoming chapters, we will discuss the pillars upon which a well-published book stands.

Chapter Four

What the HECK are All of Those Numbers?

If you have decided to join the ranks of successful self-publishers, you are about to enter a world with rules, acronyms, and organizations that might need some explaining.

Releasing a new book will entail working with book industry organizations. There will be items and details you need to know before you get started.

First, you should register your publishing company with your local secretary of state. Make sure you pick a name that reflects a larger scope than your first book or name. Do NOT register your author name anywhere as your publisher name. You will need a professional sounding name for Bowker *(www.myidentifiers.com)*, your distributor, wholesaler, or the POD companies.

"Amy Collins Press" will sound small-town and self-published. You would be better served to pick a more "global" name, such as "Capital Publications."

Once you have a name, a State-registered business number, you will need a SAN for your company, ISBNs for your publishing program, and a Library of Congress pre-control number for your first book.

First, you should apply for your own ISBN publisher prefix and plan to identify and circulate your books properly in the industry supply chain.

Every book has a unique thirteen-digit International Standard Book Number (ISBN). This number has a prefix that identifies the publisher and each number identifies a book for the entire industry.

While there are many organizations that assign ISBNs in the world, in the U.S., these numbers are assigned by R.R. Bowker.

Go to *www.myidentifiers.com* and apply today!

WHAT IS AN ISBN?

The International Standard Book Number (ISBN) is a thirteen-digit number that uniquely identifies books and book-like products published internationally.

WHAT IS THE PURPOSE OF AN ISBN?

The purpose of the ISBN is to establish and identify one title or edition of a title from one specific publisher and is unique to that edition, allowing for more efficient marketing of products by booksellers, libraries, universities, wholesalers, and distributors.

WHAT IS THE FORMAT OF THE ISBN?

Every ISBN now consists of thirteen digits. The thirteen digit number is divided into five parts of variable length, each part separated by a hyphen.

DOES THE ISBN-13 HAVE ANY MEANING IMBEDDED IN THE NUMBERS?

The five parts of an ISBN are as follows:

- The current ISBN-13 will be prefixed by "978"
- Group or country identifier that identifies a national or geographic grouping of publishers
- Publisher identifier which identifies a particular publisher within a group
- Title identifier that identifies a particular title or edition of a title
- Check digit is the single digit at the end of the ISBN which validates the ISBN

WHY DO SOME ISBNs END IN AN "X"?

In the case of the check digit, the last digit of the ISBN, the upper case X can appear. The method of determining the check digit for the ISBN is the modulus 11 with the weighting factors 10 to 1. The Roman Numeral X is used in lieu of 10 where ten would occur as a check digit.

WHO CAN ASSIGN ISBNs TO A PUBLISHER?

There are over 160 ISBN Agencies worldwide, and each ISBN Agency is appointed as the exclusive agent responsible for assigning ISBNs to publishers residing in their country or geographic territory. The United States ISBN Agency is the only source authorized to assign ISBNs to publishers supplying an address in the United States, U.S. Virgin Islands, Guam, and Puerto Rico and its database establishes the publisher of record associated with each prefix. Once an ISBN publisher prefix and associated block of numbers has been assigned to a publisher by the ISBN Agency, the publisher can assign ISBNs to publications it holds publishing rights to.

However, after the ISBN Agency assigns ISBNs to a publisher, that publisher cannot resell, re-assign, transfer, or split its list of ISBNs among other publishers. These guidelines have long been established to ensure the veracity, accuracy, and continued utility of the international ISBN standard.

As defined by the ISO Standard, the ISBN publisher prefix (or "root" of the ISBN) identifies a single publisher. If a second publisher subsequently obtains an ISBN from the assigned publisher's block of ISBNs, there will be no change in the publisher of record for any ISBN in the block as originally assigned. Therefore, searches of industry databases for that re-assigned ISBN will identify the original owner of that assigned prefix as the publisher rather than the second publisher. Discovering this consequence too late can lead to extensive costs in applying for a new prefix, re-assigning a new ISBN, and potentially leading to the application of stickers to books already printed and in circulation.

If you are a new publisher, you should apply for your own ISBN publisher prefix and plan to identify and circulate your books properly in the industry supply chain.

You may encounter offers from other sources to purchase single ISBNs at special offer prices; you should be wary of purchasing from these sources for the reasons noted above. There are unauthorized re-sellers of ISBNs and this activity is a violation of the ISBN standard and of industry practice.

A publisher with one of these re-assigned ISBNs will not be correctly identified as the publisher of record in Books In Print or any of the industry databases such as Barnes & Noble or Amazon or those of wholesalers such as Ingram. If you have questions, contact the U.S. ISBN Agency for further advice.

WHO IS ELIGIBLE FOR AN ISBN?

The ISBN Agency assigns ISBNs at the direct request of publishers, eBook publishers, audio cassette and video producers, software producers and museums and associations with publishing programs.

HOW LONG DOES IT TAKE TO GET AN ISBN?

If you go to *www.myidentifiers.com*, you get them instantly!

WHERE DO I GO TO GET AN ISBN?

- Start at *www.myidentifiers.com*
- Purchasing 10 ISBNs (the minimum) is $295
- Purchasing 100 ISBNs is $995
- Purchasing 1000 ISBNs is $1795
- Think carefully about how many ISBNs you might need over the next few years
- NOTED: The processing service charge is NON-REFUNDABLE

WHAT DO I DO WHEN I RECEIVE THE ISBN AND WHERE IS IT PRINTED?

An ISBN should be assigned to each title or product, including any backlist or forthcoming titles. Each format or binding must have a separate ISBN (i.e., hardcover, paperbound, VHS video, laserdisc, eBook format, etc.). A new ISBN is required for a revised edition. Once assigned, an ISBN can never be reused. An ISBN is printed on the lower portion of the back cover of a book above the bar code and on the copyright page.

HOW AND WHERE DO I REGISTER MY ISBN?

Once ISBNs have been assigned to products they should be reported to R.R. Bowker as the database of record for the ISBN Agency. Companies are eligible for a free listing in various directories such as Books in Print, Words on

Cassette, The Software Encyclopedia, Bowker's Complete Video Directory, etc.

NOTE: Receiving just your ISBNs does NOT guarantee title listings. To ensure your titles get in the Books in Print database you must submit your title information.

Book titles should be registered with Books in Print at *www.myidentifiers.com*.

WHAT IS A PRICE SPECIFIC ISBN AND DO I NEED ONE?

YES! Bookstores and other retailers will usually REQUIRE that books on their shelves include a barcode with the price embedded right in it.

Look on the back of the nearest book. Does the barcode have a number across the top that starts 978? That is your 13-digit ISBN (or EAN). To the right of that number should be a "5" and then 3 or 4 digits that make up the price of a book. A $16.95 book will show 51695.

If the barcode is NOT price specific, it will end 90000. This is not acceptable to most retailers and will keep you out of most stores. Get a price specific bar code!

WHAT ARE LIBRARY OF CONGRESS NUMBERS?

A Library of Congress catalog card number is a unique identification number that the Library of Congress assigns to the catalog record created for each book in its cataloged collections.

Once you have gotten your ISBN, register your book with Books in Print. At that point, it is time to send your book to the Library of Congress.

The Cataloging in Publication program creates bibliographic records for forthcoming books most likely to be widely acquired by U.S. libraries. The bibliographic record (also known as CIP data) is sent to the publisher and printed on the verso of the title page. A machine-readable version of the record is also distributed to libraries, book dealers, and bibliographic networks worldwide via the Library's Cataloging Distribution Service (CDS).

The Preassigned Control Number (PCN) program assigns a Library of Congress Control Number (aka Library of Congress Card Number) to titles most likely to be acquired by the Library of Congress as well as some other categories of books. The publisher prints the control number in the book and thereby facilitates cataloging and other book processing activities for libraries and booksellers who obtain copies of the book. An initial bibliographic record is also created for many of these works when the number is assigned. This record is not distributed and is not printed in the book. The CIP program and PCN program are mutually exclusive. Titles processed in one program are not processed in the other program.

Librarians use it to locate a specific Library of Congress catalog record in the national databases and to order catalog cards from the Library of Congress or from commercial suppliers. The Library of Congress assigns this number while the book is being cataloged. Under certain circumstances, however, a card number can be assigned before the book is published through the Preassigned Card Number Program.

The purpose of the Preassigned Control Number (PCN) program is to enable the Library of Congress to assign control numbers in advance of publication to those titles that may be added to the Library's collections. The publisher prints the control number in the book and thereby facilitates cataloging and other book processing activities. The PCN links the book to any record that the Library of Congress, other libraries, bibliographic utilities, or book vendors may create.

Please note that this is a two-step process. All publishers wanting to participate in the PCN Program must first complete and submit an Application to Participate. Upon approval, the publisher will receive an account number and password via e-mail. Then, publishers participating in the program log on to the PCN system and complete a Preassigned Control Number Application Form for each title for which a preassigned control number is requested. Based on the information provided by the publisher, Library staff preassign a control number to each eligible title. Upon receiving the number, the publisher prints it on the back of the title page (i.e., the copyright page) in the following manner: Library of Congress Control Number: 2007012345

Only U.S. book publishers are eligible to participate in the PCN program. These publishers must list a U.S. place of publication on the title page or copyright page of their books and maintain an editorial office in the U.S. capable of answering substantive bibliographic questions.

All forthcoming monographs that will be published in the United States and that are not included in the categories listed below are eligible for the PCN program. Card numbers are preassigned to works that may be selected and cataloged by the Library of Congress for its collections. Final determination of works selected and cataloged is made by selection librarians and recommending officers in compliance with Library of Congress collection development policies upon receipt of the printed book.

The following are ineligible:

- Books that are already published.
- Books which do not list a U.S. city as place of publication on the title page or copyright page. *(pcn.loc.gov)*
- Books for which Cataloging in Publication data has been (or will be) requested.
- EBooks (i.e. books published in electronic format).
- Serials. *(pcn.loc.gov)*
- Government documents.
- Items under fifty pages with the exception of genealogies and children's literature.
- Textbooks below the college level.
- Items not intended for wide distribution to libraries. *(pcn.loc.gov)*
- Religious instructional materials. *(pcn.loc.gov)*
- Expendable educational materials. *(pcn.loc.gov)*
- Transitory or consumable materials. *(pcn.loc. gov)*

- Translations except Spanish. *(pcn.loc.gov)*
- Mass market paperbacks.
- Single articles reprinted from periodicals and other serials.
- Audiovisual materials including mixed media and computer software.
- Music scores. *(pcn.loc.gov)*

There is no relationship between the PCN program and Copyright registration. The principal intention of copyright records is to document the intellectual or creative ownership of a work. The principal intention of the PCN program is to assign Library of Congress Control Numbers (LCCNs) in advance of publication to those titles that the Library may add to its collections. When printed in the book, the LCCN facilitates access to the bibliographic record for that book and thereby expedites book processing by libraries and book dealers who obtain copies of the book.

For more information concerning the Copyright Office, go to *www.copyright.gov*. To search copyright records, go to *www.copyright.gov/records*. The full contact information is:

Library of Congress
Copyright Office
101 Independence Avenue, S.E.
Washington, D.C. 20559
Phone: (202) 707-3000
E-mail: copyinfo@loc.gov

You can register your book with the Library of Congress if your publisher has more than four books published and registered.

However, there are ways around this rule. Library of Congress registration and a valid, properly formatted CIP block on your copyright page are some of the items that separate the "men from the boys" marketing wise.

If you are a small press with fewer than four titles and want the benefits of a Library of Congress Registration and a Catalog-in-Publication block, then follow these steps:

1. Make sure your publisher name is not trademarked. It does not matter if you have a publisher with a similar or identical name as someone else UNLESS it is trademarked.

   http://www.uspto.gov/trademarks/index.jsp

2. Register your publishing name and your TITLE information at Bowker. Go here: *https://www.myidentifiers.com/*. Libraries and Bookstores will look up your information on Bowker. Don't skip or skimp this step. A fully fleshed out profile and title data listing on your ISBN log will make a good impression. A poorly executed profile or title data block will make a bad one.

3. Apply to the Library of Congress for a Preassigned Control Number. Go here: *http://www.loc.gov/publish/pcn/*. From the LOC website: A Library of Congress catalog control number is a unique identification number that the Library of Congress assigns to the catalog record created for each book in its cataloged collections. Librarians use it to locate a specific Library of Congress catalog record in the national databases and to order catalog cards from the Library of Congress or from commercial suppliers. The purpose of the Preassigned Control Number (PCN) program is to enable the Library of Congress to assign control numbers in advance of publication to those titles that may be added to the Library's collections.

4. Once you have all of that done, it is time to get a CIP. A Cataloging in Publication record (aka CIP data) is a bibliographic record prepared by the Library of Congress or one of its vendors for a book that has not yet been published. When the book is published, the publisher includes the CIP data on the copyright page thereby facilitating book processing for libraries and book dealers.

It is not possible to get a CIP from the LOC if the book is Print on Demand, subsidized in any way by the author or published by a house that has published books by fewer than three separate authors.

Do not despair! You can get a CIP data block from a vendor. Libraries want the data in a specific way and you can hire someone to provide that to you. I like the folks at the Donohue Group at *http://www.dgiinc.com/pcip/*.

The following information was obtained at www.isbn.org

What is a SAN?

SAN stands for Standard Address Number. It is a unique Standard Identification Number for each address of an organization in or served by the publishing industry, which is engaged in repetitive transactions with other members of the industry in order to facilitate communications among them. It is an American National Standard -www.isbn.org/standards/home/isbn/resources/index.asp. NISO -Z39.43 - 1993 - Standard Address Number for the Publishing Industry.

What is the objective of SAN?

The objective of this standard is to establish an identification numbering system, by assigning each address within the industry a discrete code to be used for positive identification for all buying and selling transactions within the industry.

What is the reason for using the SAN?

Problems with various account numbers, such as billing errors, products shipped to the wrong points, errors in payments and returns, will be almost eliminated by using the SAN system.

In addition, the SAN eliminates a constant step in the order fulfillment or in the completion of many other types of transactions—the "look up procedure," used to assign the account numbers. Without SAN, a library or a store dealing with fifty different publishers is assigned a different account number by each supplier. SAN solves this problem. If your stores, or libraries, have the SAN on your stationery and ordering documents, vendors to whom you send your transactions do not have to check your account number and can proceed immediately to process your orders. Of course, ordering can be further facilitated if you use the ISBN.

How can I find the assigned SANs?

BookIndustryLocator.com, Bowker's SAN-based online directory, lists all SAN assignments for publishers, libraries, distributors, wholesalers, bookstores, printers, book manufacturers, etc., and includes address and contact information: *www.bookindustrylocator.com.*

What are the major SAN functions?

The SAN itself has no functional meaning as it merely defines an address. It becomes functional only in its application to activities such as purchasing, billing, shipping, receiving, paying, crediting, and refunding. It may be used for any other communications or transactions between participating organizations to which you apply it.

Each account address, if ship-to or bill-to is different, will have its own SAN.

Chapter Five

YOUR BOOK: The Right Package

It is time to get out from behind your desk and get out among the books.

You've worked hard to identify your audience and write a book that will prompt readers to spend their hard-earned money to purchase your thoughts. Though important, what you have to say on the inside will never reach those readers if you don't appeal to them with the outside. The saying "don't judge a book by its cover" seems to apply everywhere *but* the book industry.

THE LOOK OF A SUCCESSFUL BOOK

Successful books look like other successful books. Readers expect a certain look from books of certain genres. If a book looks just like the other books on the shelf, a reader will be comfortable enough with it to pick it up and give it the benefit of the doubt. Books that do not have all the same elements as the other books on the shelves do not enjoy that instant acceptance by association.

Your book cover should use current, updated fonts and colors. This does not always mean a modern look, but it does mean that old, over-used, dated fonts and colors will give your book the air of "self-published" that you want to avoid.

Your book also needs to have back cover copy and quotes that look just like all the other books' back cover copy and quotes. Properly designed book covers possess an air of sophistication no matter what they actually look like. Crocheted doilies on grandmotherly cookbook covers or knives dripping blood on mystery novels . . . no matter what the look, the feel needs to be sharp, well designed, and polished.

I am not saying that all books need to pander to the common denominator. I do not claim that all covers should be the same. Some of the most successful books ever had unusual, unique designs that broke the mold. What I am suggesting is that first-time publishers should play it a tad safe and give their first books the best shot possible.

Once you fully understand and can exhibit a polished, professionally designed cover, then you can go off the reservation. Sorry, but we all have to prove ourselves and make a name for ourselves while playing by the rules; after that, it is less risky if you want to break some of the rules.

HOW TO GET THE LOOK YOU WANT

It's not hard to learn what a properly designed, professionally published book looks like. Thanks to Amazon and the Internet, you can do much of your research from home. A lot, but not all. Your fingers won't be able to do all the walking. You also need to get your legs moving . . . up, down, and around the aisles of your local bookstore.

Internet chat rooms, industry magazines, and online bookstores can provide some good information, but if you are serious about becoming a savvy, market-driven publisher, you need to spend a great deal of time in the marketplace. It is time to get out from behind your desk and get out among the books.

When you get to the bookstore, wander up and down all the aisles . . . not just those of your favorite categories. With a pen and paper in hand, slowly pace around the store moving your head back and forth noting titles that jump out at you from the shelves. After six or seven aisles, go back and look at the books you wrote down. Were they face out? Were just the spines showing? If the books you noticed were spine-out, what do the spines have in common? Was the lettering large and easy to read? What colors were used?

Now go wander around the display tables—all the tables, not just the ones you would normally peruse. What cover do you notice first? Which books do you think about picking up? Write these titles down. Go to the next table and continue to notice your reaction. Write down the titles of the covers that draw your eye. Once you have cruised all the tables and aisles, you will have a strong list of the spines and covers that appealed to you.

Your list from the bookstore is a great way to discover what you like in a cover. The next step is to find out what the bestselling books in your category look like. This can be done online. Go to Amazon or BN.com (or both) and pull up the top-selling books in your category. Scan through the covers and see what colors are hot right now. Check out the fonts and see what the books have in common. For example, for a while, many bestselling self-help books were yellow and blue. During that same period, a majority of the bestselling business books had white covers and huge lettering.

The colors, fonts, and looks that herald an up-to-date cover change constantly. Once you have done your research, don't rest on your laurels. Return to the bookstore and check bestselling lists every month to stay current.

You have found what appeals to you and identified what a new bestselling book in your category looks like. Can you find a book on the bestseller list that has the qualities that appeal to you? Can you find two or three? Grab the covers from the Internet and make a file to later give to your cover designer.

HARDCOVER VS. PAPERBACK

According to all the book buyers I know (including the Barnes & Noble corporate buyers), the days of books having to be launched in hardcover are over. Important fiction and non-fiction are now releasing in paperback all the time.

People don't buy books in hardcover the way they used to. These days, 85 percent of the dollars spent on fiction are trade paperbacks. Factor in the price difference and this means that less than a small percentage of the fiction books sold in America are hardcover. And those are launched by big houses for established, big-name authors.

Yes, there are exceptions, but if you want to maximize your chances of stocking and sell through, you will not take the chance that you will be one of the very few exceptions. Everyone thinks that they will be different. They aren't.

I know that hardcover books are more appealing for some authors. They think of hardcovers as more legitimate. They believe the hardcover will bring in more dollars. They believe that libraries want hardcovers and think that they cannot get reviews with paperbacks. But those ideas are outdated.

Reviewers now review trade paperback fiction all the time. Libraries have less money than ever before and prefer trade paperback for new authors.

Hardcover books from new authors or small houses are rarely, if ever, stocked by major chains; therefore, sales are far less likely than in trade paper. (Example: If a Books-A-Million buyer likes a book from an established publisher, he or she might take in 150 of a hardcover versus being willing to test 800 to 1,000 of a paperback.)

A well-known fiction buyer with more than twenty-five years' experience has seen the passages of our industry and has kept himself up-to-date with the changing elements. When asked about hardcover versus paperback, he had this to say, "*With so many small presses pitching fiction today, publishers should be obsessed with placement. They cannot get placement with hardcovers. Hardcover sales are hemorrhaging. . . . Please, I'm begging you, tell your publishers to stop publishing in hardcover."*

That said, there are times when publishing a book in hardcover is a good idea. Many books are not published for the bookstore shelves. You may be publishing a book destined for corporate sales or you may be a speaker who plans to sell your book from the back of a Marriot Inn conference room. In these circumstances, publishing a book in hardcover and making the extra dollars that come from the higher price might be best.

Always keep the customer in mind when you are choosing the type of book you are going to publish. For example, if you have written a crumpet cookbook, your potential readership may prefer a book that lays open heavily and will be used and reused often enough to warrant the durability of a hardcover book. If you have written a cozy mystery, well-loved by elderly ladies, your readers may not appreciate having to hold up a big, heavy book for hours while they read.

But just like when we were doing our reader and market research, do NOT depend upon your own opinion. You are NOT your customer. If you are truly serious about publishing, you will do the research and ask many buyers their opinion on this before making your decision.

THE IDEAL PAGE COUNT

Again, you'll need to keep your readers in mind when choosing a page count range. Whether they realize it or not, readers have expectations regarding the length of a book according to genre or subject.

Take a look at those books that sell well in your genre or that cover your topic.

For instance, perhaps you are a very concise writer and managed to cram the history of the Roman Empire into a forty-page book. You may have included all the essential information a reader could want on the topic, but when your book is sitting on the shelf next to a 400-page tome about the Roman Empire, which do you think the reader will choose? The reader is going to pay a few dollars more for what he or she thinks is a great deal more information.

Maybe you've written a book about time management geared toward the busy mom. You managed to whip out a 700-page book chock-full of great ideas. I'm sorry to say that your life-altering suggestions aren't likely to ever reach that mom. If she barely has time to cook dinner for her children, do you really think she'll have time to read 700 pages?

Take a look at those books that sell well in your genre or that cover your topic. What is the average page count range? You'll want to stay in line with these books in order to appeal to the reader. So how do you figure out what your page count will be before it goes through layout? Using the following chart, divide your word count by the appropriate words-per-page to get an estimate of what your book's page count will be:

- Trade paperback (5.5 x 8.5): 310 words per page
- Mass-market paperback (4 x 7): 285 words per page
- Trade hardcover (6 x 9): 350 words per page

The page count of a book will, or at least should, play a role in determining the price of the book, which leads us to your next executive decision . . .

PRICING YOUR BOOK

How do publishers decide on a price for their books? They consider several factors: current market pricing on similar books, page count, the presence of photos, and the reputation of the author.

For example, if you have written a book about using Microsoft Word, go to the bookstore and find the books about Microsoft Word that most resemble your own. Write down the page count and price of each book. If you divide the price of each book by the page count of each, you might find that the average price per page is seven to eight cents. At that point, you should take your page count and multiply by that same number.

If you have a 300-page book at an average of seven cents per page, you have a $20.95 book. (Books usually are priced down to the ninety-five cents and ninety-nine cents below the price set.) So $20.95 is a good starting point when deciding upon your book's price, but if you want to price your book to appeal to the broadest customer base, consider a $19.99 or $24.99 price point. A potential customer makes a mental jump when a book crosses the $20 and $25 threshold.

You may be tempted to base decisions about the price, cover, and size of your book on how much you want to make off each sale. No. Nope. Don't. Nope.

Another thing to consider when setting a book's price is the potential audience. If you are publishing a book to primarily sell at the back of the rooms in which you are speaking, a lower price point is not always necessary. A higher price might not dissuade your target market.

Take into account your customer's economic situation when pricing the book. If you have written a children's book, your key consumers are parents, librarians, teachers, and in some cases, family members looking for a gift. These target consumers do not have as much disposable income as other segments of the book-buying market. As a new publisher, you should price your book at or below the price of other children's books. On the other hand, if your book is created for a corporation, a high-end, well-paid professional, or a financially fortunate demographic, then you may price your book a bit higher.

Higher priced books are not going to be suited for the bookstore market. Bookstore buyers know what their customers will spend on a book and are not interested in stocking a book priced outside of that range. But if the bookstore shelf is not your destination, then you have a bit more leeway.

SIZE OF THE BOOK—COST VS. BEAUTY

First, determine the price and packaging for your book. To do this, use books currently selling well in today's marketplace. Take pains to emulate successful books in your category that are less than two years old in order to determine the size, look, and qualities of your book.

First, add up all the costs associated with developing your book and add in the printing costs. Generally, the cost should not be more than 30 percent of the retail price. If it is, the answer is not raising the price of your book. The answer is lowering your production costs.

There are a number of ways to get the package you want at the price you should pay. Please do not try to save money by cutting the page count by choosing a smaller font size or larger trim size. Buyers can see that a mile away and will often put a book in the no pile for being a 6 x 9 when the category standard is 5 x 8.

The best ideas come from walking your local bookstores and educating yourself. Take the time to learn what current book packages look like and sell for, and you will be on your way to a marketable package.

Before we move on, I want to pass on these reminders:

- Hardcovers will not make you more money
- 6 x 9 and 7 x 10 paper sizes may save you some pages for print costs, but buyers know that trick and will refuse your book for looking self-published.
- Spiral-bound is almost NEVER a good idea. Buyers hate them because there is no spine to read and the wire bends and ruins other books.

Chapter Six

Building Your Team

All great writers have editors. One of the biggest obstacles new publishers face is the isolation that comes with the creative process. Unlike painting or sculpting, writing and publishing cannot be done alone. A written book is only half finished. It is a publisher's job to take the book the rest of the way. Building a team of book professionals is vital if you are going to move out of the "self published" arena and into the realm of bestseller.

YOUR EDITOR

A professional, experienced editor can make the difference between a well-written book and an amateurish effort. Hiring a talented editor to rework your manuscript is only the first step; you have to let them do the reworking. It is important to find an editor you trust, but it is even more important to find one you respect. Many a masterpiece was never created because a publisher let the author refuse an editor's suggestions.

When you are the author and the publisher, it is very hard. A publisher has no qualms about handing a manuscript over to a talented editor, but authors usually pale at the thought. Successful authors/publishers learn how to separate their roles, and once the author is finished, the publisher takes over.

Why Your English Teacher, Mother, Neighbor, Friend, or Church Secretary Cannot Edit or Proofread Your Book:

▶ They have not developed the years of training it takes to catch every mistake.

▶ They do not know the proper arc and format of each type of book.

▶ They do not know *The Chicago Manual of Style* standards for book publishing.

▶ Yes, they catch every spelling mistake in their daily lives, but they do not catch every spacing, line setting, page number, and margin error. They do not know what to look for.

▶ They do not have the software and computer skills to work as efficiently as a professional.

▶ They will miss things, and you will lose your chance to publish a good book and end up publishing a "could-have-been-good" book.

▶ Because I said so.

WHAT AN EDITOR DOES

Sometimes called a developmental editor, structural editor, substantive editor, or content editor, your editor's job is to view the manuscript as a whole from the reader's perspective. He or she will evaluate the manuscript's organization, tone, consistency, clarity, flow, and logic, and rework or rewrite the text as necessary. Often, the editor will also offer suggestions to the author, requesting that he or she flesh out an idea, clarify an issue, and/or resolve faulty logic.

You may have read and reread your manuscript a hundred times, but your editor will still make changes. This doesn't mean you are a poor writer; it means the editor is doing his or her job. All great writers have editors. Because you are so close to your manuscript, it is difficult for you to observe your work with an objective eye. Don't take any of the editor's changes personally. Each of you has the same goal: creating a well-written, marketable book.

DIFFERENCE BETWEEN COPY EDITORS AND PROOFREADERS

Reviewers will make up a good portion of your publicity plan. A good cover design may get your book past the first hurdle and onto a reviewer's desk. However, if your book was not professionally copy edited and proofread, it will become instantly obvious to the professional reviewer who has made a reputation and living spotting shoddy work. Your manuscript will be tossed aside.

As fabulous as your editor is, he or she is going to be focused on the manuscript as a whole, not the nuts and bolts. That's why your manuscript must move into the hands of the next member of your team, your copy editor.

WHAT A COPY EDITOR DOES

After you and your editor have made all the necessary revisions to your manuscript, you will hand it over to your copy editor. He or she is going to scrutinize every word in every line in your manuscript. The copy editor focuses on grammar, spelling, word usage, style, and clarity of writing.

Some copy editors will go above and beyond the meticulous duties inherent in the nuts and bolts of writing. For instance, he or she might also shorten or rewrite lengthy and complicated sentences, fact-check content, offer suggestions for transition sentences, and break up long paragraphs to make the text easier to read. However, you cannot expect your copy editor to rewrite the manuscript for you or check the accuracy of every statement you make. Be sure to set reasonable expectations with your copy editor and be prepared to pay more if you want things outside the realm of his or her normal duties.

WHAT A PROOFREADER DOES

Your proofreader is going to . . . you guessed it: read the proofs (the typeset book). The proofreader is your last line of defense against mistakes in the text. In some cases, he or she will check the proofs against the copy edited manuscript to ensure that all the changes have made their way into the final set. Other proofreaders read "blind"—without the use of the copy edited manuscript. The choice is yours.

The proofreader will keep an eye out for typos, repeated paragraphs, offset text, and omitted words. Design elements also come into play during this stage. Running headers, page numbers, cross-references, graphs, tables, charts, and illustrations are all checked. Essentially, your proofreader will act as a quality inspection, so do not assume you can get by without one (or two!).

YOUR COVER DESIGNER

If you are a relatively new author or publisher, you will need good reviews to give you both credence and notice. Professionally designed and edited books can clear the first hurdle at any reviewer's office . . . the assistant. It is the assistant's job to weed out the "loser" books. If your cover looks self-published and if your back cover copy does not snap with professionally written zing, you will not be sent.

A great-looking cover does not have to work as hard at convincing a reader to pick up the book.

So, to give your book a fighting chance in the ring, you need to hire a professional cover designer. Cover designers are also a highly trained, unappreciated group. There are so many great books, well edited, with lilting tones and beautiful themes, that will never grace a bookshelf because the cover was designed by a Web designer-neighbor-of-the-author-who-does-great-work.

WHAT A COVER DESIGNER DOES

Good cover design is an art and a craft. Designers work for years to learn the craft; it cannot be duplicated by those without experience. You can spot an "almost properly designed" cover a mile away. They usually have too much back cover text or a hard-to-read spine. They use inexpensive art and ubiquitous fonts. So, before hiring a cover designer, carefully peruse his or her portfolio and make sure he or she invests in current, updated fonts on a regular basis.

Let me share something with you that will make you want to drop this book, run to your computer, and fire a blistering e-mail off to my publisher, calling for my head: What your book looks like is more important than what it says.

A cover's job is to convince a shopper to pick up the book and read the back cover copy. The back cover copy's job is to convince the shopper to flip open the book and skim a few pages. The pages then have to convince the shopper to bring the book to the cash register. It all starts with the cover.

Think of a well-designed cover like the pretty girl in high school. She got all the attention. Less "well designed" girls may be funny, quirky, and totally worth the time to get to know . . . but they have to work harder to prove it. I know how unfair this is, but it's a reality we need to embrace and work with.

**"What your book looks like
is more important than what it says."**

Your cover designer is going to know what it takes to give your book that distinctive appeal, but that doesn't mean you shouldn't have any say in what your book will look like. It's time to pull out your file of covers you like (remember the market research from Chapter 4). Choose those you like best and e-mail them to your cover designer. Your cover designer needs to see what you want. While it is not a good idea to micromanage your designer, it is a good idea to provide examples to emulate. Concepts and examples will give your designer a place from which to start. Ask your designer to give you three concepts and agree upon a deadline of when you will see them.

HOW MUCH WILL YOUR TEAM COST?

A lot.

There is a wide range of options when you are deciding on your budget. The cost for editors, cover designers, production vendors, and printers necessary to complete a book will vary. There are online services that will promise to edit, proof, design, and print your book for as low as $2,000. Remember, however, you get what you pay for. These packages are "cookie cutter" and template driven. These designs are not marketplace focused, nor are they based on modern talent or research.

I hate to do it, but I find myself in the position several times a year where I have to tell hundreds of talented, hardworking strangers that they should not expect to ever see their books on a bookstore shelf. How do I know this? Because they do not have the money to hire an experienced proofreader, editor, or cover designer.

Money is tight, books are expensive, and there are no guarantees. Why on earth do any of us do this? Because we love it. Because we have learned how to publish carefully and profitably, and you can too. The key is learning where to invest your budget so that it yields the most potential sales.

Talented, experienced editors take their time and work with authors to develop the manuscript. They polish and refine good writing and will even go so far as to help rewrite less-than-good writing. They are rare jewels in our industry and not available at bargain prices. Developmental editors charge anywhere from $75 to $200 an hour, depending on their pedigree and experience. If they have edited a bestselling book, their prices will go up.

A good copy editor will charge anywhere from $15 to $35 per thousand words, depending upon how heavily he or she has to copy edit. If the copy editor has to correct a few grammar mistakes and make a few spelling corrections, a 200-page manuscript will only cost about $4 a page to copy edit. Some charge 2.5 cents a word . . . If your manuscript needs a deep edit with many rewrites on several sentences per page, you will be looking at closer to $7 to $8 a page.

Proofreaders usually charge by the hour, and depending on the manuscript and type of book, you can expect to pay $300 to $400 per proofread of a 256-page book. Always hire two proofreaders. You will need one proofreader to proof the manuscript and another to proof the book again right before you go to print for the actual book. Two sets of eyes can always catch what one set of eyes (no matter how talented) cannot.

You know how important a well-designed cover is. A designer who can give you that well-designed cover will cost $700 to $1,500.

Good editors and designers are rare jewels in our industry and not available at bargain prices.

HOW TO FIND YOUR TEAM

According to the Brenner Information Group, an industry think tank, half of the high-income small publishers earned more than $1 million in 1997 working out of home offices. Cottage industries throughout the country live and die on strong relationships and good vendors.

Finding the right people to partner with you is key in starting your publishing business. If you find the right talent at the right price, you are half way to a successful publishing plan. It takes some research, planning, and negotiating to get the best talent for the best price.

Many new publishers end up paying too much for their vendors. Others decide to go with the least expensive and get poor quality. You can avoid these traps. There are a few different ways to find potential editors and designers:

- Find books that you like and look for the editors' names on the copyright page
- Check out the best-designed covers in your genre and look for the designers' names on the copyright page
- Find great cover designers at www.creativehotlist t.com
- Find professional copy editors and proofreaders at www.mediabistro.com or the Editorial Freelancers Association at www. the-efa.org

If you're new to publishing, how will you know that the people you have chosen are doing the best possible job, and what will you do if they don't follow through on their promises?

Consider hiring a full-service book production team. Talented, experienced publishing professionals provide editors, designers, and market-savvy guidance.

WHOM TO AVOID

- Full-service companies that want to share your rights in exchange for printing your books.
- Editorial or design companies without a list of references willing to be contacted.

- Self-publishing print-on-demand companies that promise to get your books into online bookstores to be ordered one at a time. Print-on-demand titles are not eligible for stocking in bookstores because they are non-returnable.
- Consultants who charge for large packages without offering a firm timeline, references, examples, and guarantees of quality.
- Always trust your gut. If you don't have a good feeling about a prospective vendor, move on to another one.

MONEY MATTERS

- Ask the prospective vendors for an hourly or per-page quote.
- Compare prices with other vendors.
- If the vendor gives you an estimate of hours, make sure it is binding at the top end.
- Expect to pay over the estimate if you need to make changes after the project is under way.

BEFORE ANYONE GETS TO WORK

- Look for copies of the same books at bookstores and online.
- Have a team with whom you agree to share estimates before you make any decisions or sign any contracts.

It is easy to get caught up in the excitement when you meet the "right" person to add to your team, but a twenty-four-hour waiting period and outside verification will help you be more confident with your decision.

- Call at least three references for each vendor you are considering.
- Request copies of their most recent book projects.
- Take copies to your local bookstore and ask staff to evaluate the level of quality in the books.
- You should have the names and copies of three books that have the look you are hoping to emulate.
- You should acquaint yourself with the look and layouts of bestselling books in your category.

Assembling Your Pre-Press Team
—By Michele DeFilippo, owner, 1106 Design

Establishing a new publishing company is relatively easy. A much more difficult task is to assemble the team of people you'll need to properly prepare your titles for the brutal book marketplace. If you're new to publishing, it's not easy to find, evaluate, and coordinate the many providers you'll need to prepare your book for printing, especially if you are launching your new publishing business while working at a full-time job.

It's never a good idea to "do-it-yourself" when it comes to design and typesetting. If you don't have design training and experience, your results won't be acceptable to the gatekeepers of the book industry—the reviewers, distributors, and retailers you'll depend on to sell your books. But should you hire individual freelancers or larger companies who offer one-stop convenience at a higher price?

If you enjoy "getting your hands dirty" and diving into a mountain of details, then hiring individual freelancers for title writing, manuscript editing, back cover copywriting, cover design, interior design, and typesetting is the way to go. You'll spend a great deal of time coordinating all aspects of the project, but you'll have maximum flexibility and may even acquire all these services at a reduced rate, because freelancers don't have as much overhead as a larger business.

The down side is that individual freelancers are more susceptible to life events that can delay your job. And, you may not discover until it's too late that some freelancers are just not reliable or even very good at what they do. One thing is certain: Unless you already have experience in pre-press production management, you will be surprised at the amount of time it requires.

If you prefer to focus on the "big picture" business issues, then you may find it more convenient to work with a larger company that offers a variety of editorial and pre-press services under one roof. These companies assume all the headaches you'd have if you hired freelancers yourself. They offer a group of pre-qualified individuals and they manage the entire process. Naturally, this will cost more, but it's also more likely to result in a book that is finished quickly and competently while reducing your stress level significantly.

The choice you make depends on the time you have available, as well as your personal style and preferences. But understanding some of the issues you're likely to encounter should make the decision an easier one.

▶ Michele DeFilippo is the owner of 1106 Design, LLC, which offers one-stop editorial and book design services to publishers large and small, with hand-holding. For more information, visit www.1106design.com or contact Michele at md@1106design.com.

Chapter Seven

The Publishing Process

It will be the writing, and the writing alone, that is judged worthy or not. Books start with the writing, and if the publishing process is handled correctly, that is where books should end as well. It is the poorly published books that end up on the scrap heap and never get read. Don't let beautiful writing get ignored or discarded because of poor publishing.

You have assembled your team, checked all their references, seen some of their work, and compared their efforts to books on the bookstore shelf. As a publisher, your first job is to create a book of quality. Your second job is to create a book on time.

HOW LONG WILL IT TAKE?

The biggest mistake new publishers make is thinking that they need to get their book "out there" immediately. Publishing a successful book takes time and attention to detail. Rushing through any step of the process will inevitably harm your end result. You simply cannot rush through the book industry's set deadlines and prerequisites. Some of these processes are:

- Getting an ISBN
- Registering your book with the Library of Congress and getting a Catalog in Publication Block created for the copyright page (three weeks)
- Adding your book to Amazon.com and other industry databases (two to three weeks)
- Getting signed up with a distributor or wholesale fulfillment partner (three to four months)
- Meeting the presentation deadlines at bookstores for new books (five to six months after you are signed up with the distributor or wholesaler)
- Printing and shipping new books (three to four weeks if no issues or "fixes") or setting up POD files

Setting a realistic timeline will be your first big test as a new publisher. Do this properly and everything else will go more smoothly. This step is where we separate the wheat from the chaff, the mice from the . . . well, you get the idea.

But what about the other elements? How long does it take to design a cover? Edit a manuscript? Proofread a set of pages? While these things vary, there are some guidelines you can use to start. The following are rules of thumb and only to be used to help you start planning. When you assemble your team, you should discuss your time expectations and include them in the agreements.

- Editing and copy editing (two months)
- Getting a good cover designed (four to six weeks)
- Proofreading (two weeks)
- Laying out the finished book interior (three to four weeks with proofread changes)

With written commitments from your editors, designers, artists, authors, and proofreaders, you should be able to create a well-published book in eight months from a finished manuscript. Some people can do it in less, but if you want good reviews, strong sales possibilities, and an ulcer-free stomach, sit down and map out a schedule starting eight months out from your official pub date.

There are a number of "dates" in this process. Let's go through them so that there is no confusion. A "print date" is the date that the book comes off the printer and is shipped to the publisher. A "ship date" is the date that the publisher ships the books to its customers to fill waiting orders. This is usually two to three weeks after the print date. A "pub date" is the official date a book is available for ordering or purchasing to the general public. It is usually five to eight weeks after the ship date to give retailers time to order, receive, and shelve the books.

You need to create a realistic pub date for your book and make sure you can meet it.

It takes time to get a book from the printer to a warehouse, from a warehouse to a distributor, from a distributor to a wholesaler, from a wholesaler's receiving dock to its shelves, from a wholesaler's shelves to a bookstore, and from the back room of a bookstore to the floor.

So what does this mean to your publishing program? It means you need to create a realistic pub date for your book and make sure you can meet it. It means that you need to have a large chunk of the book finished and the publicity and marketing plans created at least six months prior to your pub date. It means that you have to set and adhere to a schedule.

BUILDING YOUR SCHEDULE

As you build your schedule for a book, add a great deal of "cushion" into the schedule. There will be miscommunications, vendor problems, production errors, shipping mishaps—all resulting in delaying your book's debut to the world. If you build in enough time to deal with the inevitable delays, you will always be "on time." You will have a lot less stress. And it's definitely worth it.

Let's walk through a sample schedule. If you announce that you will be publishing *I Was a Teenage Latte Addict* in early October, your book should leave the printer no later than early August. Plan accordingly and work up the schedule so you don't get worked up later.

The following ideas are just a starting point. I have left room for you to fill in your own "to-do"s.

Eight months before publication of
I Was a Teenage Latte Addict:

☐ Editors, pre-production team, and cover designer hired
☐ Book manuscript is finished and given to the editor
☐ ISBN is assigned
☐ Title, subtitle, and tag lines are decided upon
☐ Decisions on which distributor to use made
☐ Decide if POD is the best distribution and print option for your book
☐ Marketing and sales plan created
☐ Cover design concept meeting held with designer

☐ _____

☐ _____

☐ _____

☐ _____

☐ _____

☐ _____

☐ _____

Seven months before publication of
I Was a Teenage Latte Addict:

- ☐ Cover design work continues
- ☐ Back cover copy written
- ☐ One-page book description written
- ☐ Page count decided upon
- ☐ Hard/soft cover decided upon
- ☐ Price decided upon
- ☐ Register book with R.R. Bowker and Library of Congress

☐ _____

☐ _____

☐ _____

☐ _____

☐ _____

☐ _____

☐ _____

☐ _____

Six months before publication of
I Was a Teenage Latte Addict:

☐ Developmental edit finished and given to copy editor
☐ Front cover design close to finished

☐ _____

☐ _____

☐ _____

☐ _____

☐ _____

☐ _____

☐ _____

☐ _____

☐ _____

☐ _____

Five months before publication of
I Was a Teenage Latte Addict:

☐ Copy edit finished and sample pages designed
☐ Book specs sent to wholesalers, distributors, and bookstores
   (including Amazon)
☐ First pass layout of book done
☐ Proofread PDFs of your book layout
☐ Proofread PDFs of your book cover

☐ _____

☐ _____

☐ _____

☐ _____

☐ _____

☐ _____

☐ _____

☐ _____

Four months before publication of
I Was a Teenage Latte Addict:

☐ Digitally print fifty copies of Advanced Reader's Copies (ARCs) of your book for marketing purposes and to give your project a "dry run"

☐ Send copies of the ARCs to reviewers and websites for endorsements and reviews

☐ _____

☐ _____

☐ _____

☐ _____

☐ _____

☐ _____

☐ _____

☐ _____

☐ _____

Three months before publication of
I Was a Teenage Latte Addict:

☐ "Live with" your ARC for a few weeks
☐ Do a final proofread and make any final changes and adjustments
☐ Send final PDFs to the printer

☐ _____

☐ _____

☐ _____

☐ _____

☐ _____

☐ _____

☐ _____

☐ _____

☐ _____

Two months before publication of
I Was a Teenage Latte Addict:

☐ Books ship from printer to warehouse

☐ Send copies of finished book to your entire team with thank-you notes

☐ Send copies of your finished book to the bookstores and retailers whom you wish to consider stocking your book

☐ Send copies of your finished book to stores and contact them about doing an event during your pub month or the month after

☐ _____

☐ _____

☐ _____

☐ _____

☐ _____

☐ _____

☐ _____

One month before publication of
I Was a Teenage Latte Addict:

☐ Books start to ship from retailers to readers
☐ Google and search engine set up to find all mentions for your clipping files
☐ Approach Amazon Top Reviewers for reviews
☐ Approach bloggers and book clubs for reviews
☐ Send copies of your finished book to the bookstores and retailers whom you wish to consider stocking your book

☐ _____

☐ _____

☐ _____

☐ _____

☐ _____

☐ _____

☐ _____

☐ _____

Month of publication of
I Was a Teenage Latte Addict:

☐ Approach Amazon Top Reviewers for reviews
☐ Send copies of your finished book to the bookstores and retailers whom you wish to consider stocking your book

☐ _____

☐ _____

☐ _____

☐ _____

☐ _____

☐ _____

☐ _____

☐ _____

☐ _____

☐ _____

One month after publication of
I Was a Teenage Latte Addict:

☐ Approach bloggers and book clubs for reviews
☐ Send copies of your finished book to the bookstores and
  retailers whom you wish to consider stocking your book
☐ Approach Amazon Reviewers for reviews

☐ _____

☐ _____

☐ _____

☐ _____

☐ _____

☐ _____

☐ _____

☐ _____

☐ _____

Two months after publication of
I Was a Teenage Latte Addict:

☐ Approach bloggers and book clubs for reviews

☐ Send copies of your finished book to the bookstores and retailers whom you wish to consider stocking your book

☐ Approach Amazon Reviewers for reviews

☐ Books shipped to wholesalers and retailers that have placed orders

☐ Start sending out weekly ideas to newspapers and magazines with ideas of articles they could write (or let you write) that ties in with your book

☐ _____

☐ _____

☐ _____

☐ _____

☐ _____

☐ _____

☐ _____

Notes

Chapter Eight

Setting a Budget

The budgeting process can be a very difficult yet rewarding time in your business planning. Too many publishers start out with an unrealistic idea of saving money by doing it all themselves. As I hope you now know, it is important to let the professionals do what they do best. It is in the best interest of your book to budget for their services. So, let's take a look at a sample budget to get you started on your own.

Are you going with POD? Printing digitally? Offset? Warehousing? Using a fulfillment house? Let's use an example and walk through the possibilities.

Book:
I Was a Teenage Latte Addict,
256 pages, trade paperback,
no photos or art,
four-color cover

FIRST, THE PUBLISHING COSTS:

Publishing Element	Low End	High End
Cover	$700	$2,500
Interior design	$50	$5,000
Editing	$800	$3,800
Proofreading	$600	$1,200
eBook Creation	$0	$800

THEN, THE ADMIN AND PRINTING COSTS:

ISBN and admin costs	$400–$600
Digital printing of 500 books	$2,200–$4,000
If you go with POD proofs and set up	$100
CIP Block for copyright page	$80–$150
Barcode	$0–$50

You aren't finished once your book is printed! You still have a few more items to budget for:

- Warehousing your books
- Fulfillment costs
- Sales and marketing materials
- Sales and marketing outreach
- Shipping your books
- Promotional costs

WAREHOUSING AND STORAGE

Are you going to put your books in your garage? Guest room? Are you going to fulfill large orders from wholesalers and retailers? If so, seek out and negotiate warehouse space with a local company. They can pack and ship the orders you receive much more effectively and save you time and money. Expect to pay $25 to $50 a month in administration fees plus fifteen to thirty cents per book—or in business terms, unit—a month in storage.

FULFILLMENT

If your books are in a warehouse, the staff there will be responsible for packing and shipping your books. You can budget for about $3 to $5 per order in "pick and pack" costs. These costs are less frightening when you remember that most orders are for multiple books. If you are focusing your sales and marketing efforts to individuals and online instead of to retail and wholesale customers, consider an alternate means of storing and shipping your books. In that case, your guest room might be a good option.

SALES AND MARKETING MATERIALS

You should have a colorful, one-page sheet touting the benefits and ordering information to be sent to your prospective customers. Most stores do not want their mailbox stuffed with these, so print a small amount to start. (The printing of these sheets averages fifty cents per sheet.) If you are considering printing postcards and sending them to librarians, bookstore managers, and/or corporations, make sure you do your research and find out from representatives from each type of company what they DO with these mailers!

E-mails are a great option and cost less than printed materials, but you will still have to pay to rent the lists and you do not want to be labeled a "spammer."

Sample copies (Advance Reader's Copies or ARCs) of your book will cost approximately $6 a unit but are imperative if you want to get a review or endorsement for your book.

I always budget for at LEAST 200 free copies of each title to be given away in the first few months.

Remember . . . nothing sells a book like a book!

SALES AND MARKETING OUTREACH

Once you have your sales materials, how are you going to get the word out? Hiring someone to do your Internet outreach, postage on printed materials, and a publicist to create and pitch your message to the press are all necessary costs of your book launch. The general rule of thumb is that publishers should budget $2 a unit for every unit they plan to sell. For example, if you want to sell 1,000 books, budget $2,000 to get those books sold.

Publicists do a great job with booking authors, but cost from $5,000–$40,000 to launch a book properly. (We will discuss doing it yourself in a later chapter . . . BREATHE.)

SHIPPING

The industry standard at the current time demands that you pay for shipping to any and all retailers and wholesalers. Most publishing companies can still get away with charging shipping and handling to consumers, but if you are focusing on selling mainly through the retailers and wholesalers, it will mean you pay the freight. Budget up to 20 percent of your book's net profits for shipping. Depending on where your books are warehoused, the costs may be as low as 3 percent.

So all of these costs have to be factored in before you even start promoting the book!

How are you going to get the word out?

PROMOTIONS

If you are focusing your sales efforts on the national chains and wholesalers, you may be allowed to participate in a promotional program. Chains charge to put your book on a table or in a themed display. It is common to spend $3,000 to $5,000 in "co-op funds" to put 2,000 books on a display.

Wholesalers have a number of great programs designed to get your book in front of the biggest book buyers and librarians in the country. These programs cost anywhere from $200 for a catalog annotation to several thousand for a full, seasonal program of print, galley, and online outreach.

WHAT ABOUT POD COSTS?

The big question I hear every day: *"How much will I make per book?"*

Fair question. I can use an example to help you determine the math and figure out to the penny how much you will make.

Let's go back to our book, *I Was a Teenage Latte Addict*, 256 pages, trade paperback, 5 x 8 trim-size, no photos or art, and a four-color matte cover.

Printing the book digitally at IngramSpark will cost .015 cents per page. *IWATLA* will cost $3.84 for the interior and an additional .90 cents for the paperback cover. Total? $4.74.

If I wanted to make it a hardcover, it would still cost $3.84 for the interior, but then add an additional $7.55 for the hardcover and jacket. Total would be $11.39 to print.

IngramSpark ships the book without charging you shipping when you use their printing services. So there are no shipping costs.

If you want your book to be bought by bookstores, retailers and libraries, you HAVE to offer it a full 55 percent discount to Ingram. So my $16.95 retail price for *IWATLA* means I sell it to Ingram for $7.63.

Subtract the $4.74 printing price and I am left with a profit of $2.89 per book.

That is a GREAT profit for a small press!

But remember, from that $2.89 you need to pay for your editors, designers, and marketing costs. The first few thousand books will not end up in your bank balance. . . . But that is okay!

If you budgeted properly, you are on your way to a very successful book!

Chapter Nine

Marketing and Publicizing Your Book

You have written and slaved over your book for months, you have taken on the arduous process of learning and working as a publisher. So . . . you're done now, right? Wrong.

Many author/publishers make the mistake of thinking that once they have produced a great book, it will "sell itself." It won't. Never does. Books are remarkably little help in selling themselves. A great cover will help tremendously, a good story also will be a plus . . . but to make the difference between a good book in your garage and a good book on your neighbors' nightstands, you need marketing and publicity.

There are a number of different ways to market and publicize your book, but before we go into that, let's develop a working definition of what marketing and publicity are.

Marketing is the act of advertising, promoting, and announcing your book to a specific industry and consumer base. Marketing includes postcard mailings to librarians, ads in local movie theaters before the main show, newspaper ads in Sunday supplements, front-of-store tables at bookstores, placement ads in catalogs, and other promotional activities.

Online marketing is very popular and effective right now. It is not as driven by ads, but by outreach and "impressions" on other Internet users. What online marketing saves in dollars, it makes up for in time commitments. We will address the particulars in a moment.

Publicity, or "public relations," is the act of securing press for an author or book. Never paid for, publicity is what will get you on *Good Morning America* or into your local newspaper's Lifestyle section. A good publicist will work with editors, writers, producers, and booking staff to get your book and your name out to radio listeners, television audiences, newspaper readers, and magazine subscribers. They will help you craft your message and then disseminate it to the press.

The difference between marketing and public relations is this; If, during the six o'clock news, the anchor reads a story about your book, that is PR. If, during the six o'clock news, a commercial about your book airs between newscasts, that is marketing.

WHAT IS AN ARC?

Many times in this book, we have talked about Advance Reader's Copies. ARCs are a necessary part of your marketing plan. An ARC is an "almost" final version of your book printed with a color version of your cover used to show the press and buyers what your book will be. It is not perfect and those that receive ARCs accept that there will be minor mistakes. However, it is a supposed to give the industry a chance to read your book and see your packaging. Reviewers can review your book in advance and buyers can decide on advance orders if you have an ARC.

You can use the Write 2 Print software to layout your ARC and have your cover designer come up with a preliminary cover. On the back cover should be all the key information about your book: ISBN, release date, price, page count, trim size, marketing plans, PR plans, contact information for ordering, marketing, and press.

BOOKSTORE AND AUTHOR TOUR

One of the best ways for an author to get their message out to their community and region is to do author signings. Booking a signing does take a bit of finesse. To start, know that bookstores need ninety days' advance notice to properly book and promote a signing. Do yourself a favor and do not call your local bookstore asking to do a signing in three weeks. They have calendars and newsletters printed each month, and you need to respect their deadlines.

Next, most bookstores will not be able to book you for an event unless your books are available to order from a wholesaler or in their system. So, don't call to ask to do an event until you know that your books are available to order from a wholesaler.

Finally, to better increase your chance of selling books, don't just do a signing; plan an event. Sitting at a table for two hours can be a tad disheartening. Draw a crowd by reading, speaking, or giving a workshop.

Also, plan a launch party near the publication month at a local bookstore. Most bookstores would be thrilled to host an event for a local author because they often invite a large group of friends and family to attend. For a launch party to be successful, you need to send out invitations three weeks in advance, plan the evening around a reading or talk, and make sure you have someone there to take pictures!

Good pictures of happy people milling around a signing are an invaluable tool for your next event booking. Store managers want to know that you can draw an audience, work a room and, in general, make your event "worth their time." Make sure you have a few pictures as proof that your events are fun, crowded, and profitable.

I want to reiterate. This is a terrific way to get the word out regionally. Book events and signings create a good reason to reach out to the press and get attention for your book.

They are not, however, a good long term strategy for marketing. National author tours or doing events in distant towns will just drain your bank balance and not increase your sales. Go local and then go home. There are better ways to market yourself outside of your hometown.

PUBLICITY AND MARKETING

Do it yourself or hire a professional? Working with a professional PR or marketing firm is a big commitment. It takes time, money, and a firm understanding of your goals and your book's potential. Many authors hire professional PR and marketing consultants for help getting the word out about their books.

Unless your publishing venture has the personnel, support, and sophistication to handle its own publicity, it is almost always best to hire an experienced book PR or marketing firm to handle your initial launch and first few months of publicity and marketing.

The most powerful tools available are personal contacts, a deep understanding of the deadlines and submissions process, and knowledge of what works and what doesn't based on recent experience. Before you hire a PR professional, be comfortable that they have these tools in their toolbox.

But how do you decide if your book is ready for a PR and marketing campaign?

- Is the info in your book time sensitive?
- Does the topic of your book touch upon current events?
- Can it be "hooked" to other news, legislation, milestones, or anniversaries?
- Is your book national or local?

- Is there sufficient evidence that your book will garner good reviews?
- Do you have the time to work with your PR company?

If, after evaluating your PR potential, you would like to find a company to assist you in garnering reviews, articles, interviews, and online buzz, make sure you find one that shares your views on the industry and your topic. Too many times, authors will hire PR firms that do a great job, but do not "fit" with the message of the book, and the efforts are disappointing.

Here's an example. A vegetarian cookbook author hires a slick, aggressive urban PR firm to help launch her book *A Small Diet for Vegans without Cars*. The PR staff is talented and has tons of contacts at all the top gourmet magazines and cooking shows, but the author is constantly disappointed by the radio interviews and small blurbs her book garners. Why? Because they are pitching the book to the wrong people. A book like this will do very well with the regional environmental papers, the online networks for vegans, the New Age papers, and the local NPR stations. *A Small Diet for Vegans without Cars* does not belong on 99.5-drive-time-in-the-morning-with-potty-mouth-shock-jock. Find a PR firm that can match your message.

When hiring a consultant to help you with PR and marketing, it is advisable to set goals and deadlines:

- How long will the campaign be?

- What you want accomplished (three to four national media hits, eight local hits?)
- Your target audience reached
- Scope of the campaign (local, regional, online, national)
- At what point in the campaign shall results be evaluated?

Make sure you shop around and get real answers to your questions. There are no guarantees with PR or marketing campaigns, but there should be clear goals and parameters before you sign on the dotted line.

Things to ask your marketing or PR company before you sign:

- Do they understand your book and the potential market?
- What are their media contacts and which ones would they suggest you start with? (This will be in generalities, they will not be handing over their Rolodex, but you should expect a list of the publications and media outlets they plan to solicit.)
- Can you see copies of past reviews and articles from their client list?
- May you have a list of references? (Make sure it includes at least two current clients and two former.)
- What are your online media plans for the project?

- Will they help you come up with creative ideas and topics or is that left to you?
- How many different versions of your message are they willing to disseminate?

HOW MUCH SHOULD IT COST?

Rates vary from firm to firm, so it is important to set a budget before contacting a number of consultants asking for quotes. Know what you can afford and be up front with them. There is no set formula for what a consultant will charge and what you get for the money. You can expect to spend a minimum of $5,000 for a book launch. Add in much more if you want reviews and national television. At a minimum, you want your PR person placing and pitching stories, producing the press kit, and arranging interviews.

It is always advisable to get an "out clause" if the results are not what you agree to within the evaluation time period you have set.

Marketing and PR costs will depend upon:

- How long you need their help
- What you ask them to do for you
- What you are willing to do for yourself
- Size and prominence of the firm you are hiring
- The scope (national vs. local)

A GOOD PR OR MARKETING FIRM WILL HELP YOU:
- Craft your message for the press and marketplace

- Create your media plan and materials
- Do the research and background work on your message's relevance to current events
- Write or edit an opinion editorial to be distributed to the press
- Make pitch calls to reporters, book you on radio and television where possible
- Launch and maintain an Internet and online presence

ONLINE

Entire forests are being destroyed to supply Internet experts with the paper to write articles about how to market on the Internet, and there is still no "right" way to go about it.

Go to people's blogs and get into a discussion about their blog topics.

There are, however, a few online habits that have been proven to increase awareness of a book or message:

Comment on people's blogs. Go to people's blogs and get into a discussion about their blog topics. See who else is there and visit their blog. Do not hype your book or make a "drive by" comment. Really participate and once you are in the flow, mention your book and include a link to your page or Amazon.com.

Get out there and network. Social networking (Twitter, Pintrest, Google+, Instagram, Facebook, LinkedIn) is a great way to get your message out to people. Many sites have book discussion groups or recommendation tools.

Groups or discussions. Online forums are filled with people who are discussing your topic. Get in there and meet people, join the discussion, offer to send the leader of the forum a copy of your book.

Find popular newsletters, websites and blogs and offer the editor a guest article. You can give the editor what they need, content and get the word out about your message at the same time!

Posting on your own blog is great, but why not offer advice and guidance on a site that is FAR more trafficked and popular than yours?

Make sure you review and participate in book site discussions. Goodreads, Shelfari, Librarything. . . . Any and all sites dedicated to books should get your attention a few times a week.

HOW MUCH SHOULD YOU PAY FOR A REVIEW?

A lot of small press, print-on-demand, and self-published authors want to know where is the best place to get their books reviewed. The answers range from the biggies (*USA Today, Publisher's Weekly, Kirkus, Foreword, People,* and major newspapers such as *NY Times*) to the not so big (reader blogs, online retail sites such as Amazon, Midwest Book Review, local papers).

"Do reviews help sales?"

YES! Yes they do.

"When should an author pay for a review?"

Never. Ever. Nope. Nada. Don't. Just stop there.

If you truly want to be taken seriously by the major names in book reviews, then print some Advance Copies four months before the publication date of your book and send them out under your publisher name with a well-written cover letter, a press release, a marketing plan and a fully fleshed out list of sales and PR activities scheduled. This will give you the bare minimum introduction to the reviewers and give you a CHANCE at a review from one of the biggies.

If you cannot see yourself giving the book the three to four-month window that the major reviewers require, then you are choosing to forgo the chance of those reviews. As a small press owner, be aware that getting reviewed by these folks is about as likely as winning the lottery. If you choose to skip them, it is very similar to deciding not to buy that $400 Million Powerball ticket.

In the last year, I have had self-published, single-title authors reviewed by *Publisher's Weekly,* the *Wall-Street Journal* and *Fast Company.* These are HUGE names and the reviews drove sales (even the negative ones . . .). But these author/publishers were in the teeeeeeeeny minority. They won the lottery.

Where does the money come in? *Foreword, Kirkus,* and *Publisher's Weekly* all offer small press/print-on-demand authors a chance to get a review by paying for a listing or review in their "small press" divisions. These are valid and worthy divisions of good companies.

A reviewer's time is valuable. It is coin and worth a great deal. I am not saying that they SHOULD NOT charge for their time . . . I am saying that you should not PAY for it.

If your book is worthy of a reviewer's time, they will offer it. If you follow a reviewer's submission guidelines and respect their process, you will have a chance at getting some of their valuable time in the form of a review.

I can understand why some companies would charge for a review, but I am here to tell you that the bookstores, retail buyers and librarians who use reviews to make decisions KNOW WHICH REVIEWS WERE PAID FOR (and they disregard those reviews almost entirely).

AND, none of these "pay for consideration" divisions offer a GOOD review for money, just a chance to be reviewed.

Kirkus gives straightforward reviews to both paid and non-paid submissions (They are known for being honest to the point of brutal . . .).

Publisher's Weekly does not guarantee a review for their small-press listing fee, they just offer a better chance at a review in their small press quarterly.

This business model is not like the "fast pass" on the highway or at an amusement park. You are not paying to get bumped to the head of the line. You are exchanging your money for a review you would not likely get otherwise. Buyers and librarians know this.

Get the review the proper way, or don't bother.

As a former book buyer and as a current soldier on the front lines of the retail battlefield, I can tell you that numerous, positive, proper reviews from smaller venues help more than a paid for consideration from a bigger name.

Those that know the *Kirkus* name will know if you paid for the review and those that don't know the *Kirkus* name won't be impressed by the review. SO WHY pay for it?

Chapter Ten

Selling Your Book

There are a number of different places where books are sold. They are sold to libraries, bookstores, gift stores, corporations, catalogs, Internet retailers, audiences of speaking engagements, schools, and anywhere readers may be found. Publishers sell their books to people the author knows, people who belong to the same organizations as the author, companies that have expressed a need for the book's information, organizations that want to resell the book as a fundraiser, and retailers that believe they will have a big enough demand to warrant the risk of putting the book on their shelves.

Sales is the act of getting a store or retail venue to stock your book. Marketing is the act of letting the end user, the reader, know that your book is available and where to find it. Successful books merge both sales and marketing in a manner that results in a reader purchasing your book and taking it home.

MAKING YOUR STATEMENT

To create a truly effective sales and marketing plan, start with the who, what, where, when, why, and how.

- Who will actually shell out the money to buy your book? Outline their age, finances, gender, and circumstances.
- What makes your book worth the consumer's dollars?
- Where will your readers find your book?
- When will your readers need your book? At what point in their lives will they need your book?
- Are you sure?
- Why is your book more appealing than others in the same category? (Be brutally honest here. Do you compete on price? Is your information more up to date?)
- Are you sure?
- How will your potential readers find out about your book?

YOUR POSITIONING STATEMENT

Get all this down on paper and look at it. You are now prepared to write your book's positioning statement. When you are ready to present your book to the world (readers, bookstores, publicists, buyers, etc.), the most important tool in your arsenal will be the positioning statement. This statement is 100 words that outline for a potential buyer the reasons why your book will be of interest to their clients. These 100 words should not outline what your book is about. This statement exists to talk about the potential market for your book and how you, as the publisher, plan to reach that market.

For example, if you have identified your core readership as business executives looking for a new job, your positioning statement could look something like this:

Shut Up and Hire Me is a step-by-step program designed for the busy business executive. Each chapter was written and designed to be read in less than ten minutes. Unlike other career guides on the shelf today, *Shut Up and Hire Me* draws from the wisdom and experience of CEOs from more than thirty Fortune 500 companies. Interviews, combined with proven techniques, are provided to help executives find and land their next position. Author Bill Billiam has hired top New York PR firm, Blown Out of Proportion, and is the author of such previous works as: *Better Dead than Unemployed* and *More Money for Less Work*.

YOUR MARKETING STATEMENT

When you have your positioning statement done, then it is time to write your marketing statement. The following example would garner the attention of any buyer:

Shut Up and Hire Me has recently received several rave reviews from *Business Week, USA Today* and MSN Careers. This step-by-step program will be publicized in all the top business magazines and advertised in all major market newspapers. Bill Billiam is the host of *Business with Billiam* on Fox 5 NYC from 2:00 to 2:30 M–F and has a commitment from the *Today Show* for a three-minute segment on their morning telecast.

YOUR SALES KIT

Stores have a person or a team of people whose job is to choose the books that go on their shelves. They are "buyers."

Publishers have one chance to convince these buyers to put their books on their shelves and to do that, you must send them a complete sales kit. This includes, but is not limited to, a cover, a complete outline of the book, your positioning and marketing statements, a few sample chapters, and a one-page sheet listing all the book's pertinent information.

When selling a book to the bookstores, libraries, and chains, remember that the people seeing your book sales kit see hundreds of sales kits a day. They will choose a very small percentage of the books they see. Your kit can make the difference between a purchase order and a politely worded e-mail (We regret to inform you . . .).

Here is a complete checklist of what is recommended for a sales presentation kit for your buyers:

- [ ] Color print of the cover on heavy, glossy paper
- [ ] A bound ARC if the book is finished; sample chapters printed out if it is not.
- [ ] Fully outlined marketing and publicity plan

One-page title information sheet with:

- [ ] ISBN
- [ ] Title and Subtitle
- [ ] Author
- [ ] Author bio
- [ ] Author hometown
- [ ] 100-word description of book
- [ ] Order contact information
- [ ] Book category
- [ ] Retail price
- [ ] Page count
- [ ] Trim size
- [ ] Ship date
- [ ] Publication date
- [ ] Format
- [ ] Print run
- [ ] Co-op and advertising budget
- [ ] Title and ISBN of previous books by author or in the series
- [ ] Title and ISBN of books similar to yours

Here is an example of a title information sheet for a bookstore:

ISBN: 9780989142601

Page Count: 231

Trim: 6 x 9

Format: Paperback

Price: 14.95

Publish Date: April 10, 2013

Subject: Christian/Fantasy

Publisher: Roberts Court Reporters

Available from: Ingram or Baker & Taylor

FULLY RETURNABLE

www.newshelves.com

20 Office Parkway

Suite 126

Pittsford, NY 14534

For more information:

Amy Collins

518-261-1300

amy@newshelves.com

Seventh Dimension – The Door
A Young Adult Christian Fantasy
by Lorilyn Roberts

About the Book

For every child who struggles with doubt, for every kid who has been bullied, for every teen who comes from a broken home, and for every young adult who longs to be understood - there is hope.

Best-selling author Lorilyn Roberts shares once again the power of redemption in this Christian coming-of-age novel. Written in first-person, Seventh Dimension - The Door reads as a first-hand account by a young girl, Shale Snyder, who is treated unfairly by her family, school, and classmates. Fear distorts her sense of self-worth and she is enveloped with guilt because of a secret from her past.

While on a sojourn similar to Christian in Pilgrim's Progress, Shale discovers talking animals and a handsome young man with whom she falls in love. Her journey is one of self-discovery as she battles personal demons, family conflict, wicked underlings, and comes face-to-face with a personal decision she must make - bound up in the king she meets in first century Israel.

About the Author

Lorilyn Roberts lives in Gainesville, Florida, with her two daughters from Nepal and Vietnam. Manish's and Joy's adoption stories were told in her bestselling memoir Children of Dreams. Part of her family's memoir was featured on Discovery Channel's "Monsters Inside Me."

Marketing

- Full scale National Radio, TV and Print Media Campaign
- Online and Print Review Campaign
- National Book Chain Campaign
- Public Library Campaign
- Online Blog and Librarian Outreach
- Online Media and Optimization Campaign

Comparative Titles

- This Present Darkness (978-1581345285)
- Edge of Eternity (978-1578562954)
- The Lion, The Witch, and the Wardrobe (978-0064404990)
- A Wrinkle in Time (978-0312367541)
- Pilgrim's Progress (978-1893345904)

THE BUYERS' BUDGET AND SCHEDULE

The world of books and retail runs on dates and deadlines. You may have the best dating book in the history of the world. It may be the one program that will find true love for anyone who reads it. You may have a personal note from Oprah saying that it changed her life. None of that matters if you do not follow the schedules set by the retailers and wholesalers carrying that book to the people.

Buyers require that publishers present their books five to six months before publication. These stores have very tight budgets, and only allow a buyer to purchase as many books as they can afford in a given month. No matter how much buyers may like a book, if they have spent their budget for that month, they cannot buy it. You may ask, "Why can't they just move the book out a month and buy the next month?" Well, they can. But they often won't. If buyers start "borrowing" from future months, it only takes a few months of playing fast and loose with budgets for the whole system to get muddled up, and they will very likely lose their jobs. They like their jobs. A lot.

To be fair to everyone, a buyer has to buy a book in the month that you, the publisher, declare as the publishing date. You set that date, and you (usually) have to live with it. If your book is not coming together as quickly as you had hoped or if you are late getting the information to the buyer, it would be wise to move the pub date out to the six-month mark. I know you want to see your book(s) published and available as soon as possible, but not following the correct procedure will doom your project to a future on a few local bookstore shelves and being pitched on the Internet. If you want a chance at a real, national release, you have to follow the rules.

Every buyer is required to buy books within a set budget and schedule. Asking a buyer to find money for your book in May when his or her budget is already spent through October will not go well. Work within the system. It shows knowledge of the buyer's predicament and a respect for his or her constraints.

Are there exceptions? All the time. Should you count on being one of those exceptions? No. Exceptions to these schedules and budget timelines are created only when a book gets huge national TV or magazine exposure (*Ellen, People, USA TODAY* . . . not your local Fox morning show or the Mensa Bulletin), or when there is sufficient reason to convince buyers to go to their bosses and prove that your book is worth going outside the lines. These buyers see hundreds of new books a day. Do not count on getting their attention long enough to make your case. Just follow the rules, and it will make everyone happy.

Once buyers gather all the information on all the books scheduled for a particular month, they will go through and evaluate each on its merits, marketability, and salability. At that point, they choose the books they want and compare their list of books with the amount of money they have budgeted for that month and see if they can buy all the books they liked. They won't be able to. They never have the space or money to buy every book that they think has merit.

Now comes the sad process of skipping books that might have done well because there is another book that they believe will do better. Sometimes, they won't skip the book altogether; they will cut the number of stores that will carry the book down to just the author's hometown to see how it sells there. If they can prove to their bosses that your book has potential by seeing big sales locally, that is often a good way to get them to eventually take in more.

We already set up a schedule, but let's drill down to the sales process and see if we can add to what we already have to your already overloaded "to do" list. (Sorry!)

CREATING YOUR SALES SCHEDULE

We will be discussing the sales process later, but let's take a look at the items you will want to cover in the months leading up to your publication. This schedule is the IDEAL schedule, but please do not panic if you are releasing in three months, just do these items when you can.

SIX MONTHS BEFORE YOUR BOOK'S PUB DATE:

- Send your book's data to the wholesalers, retailers, Internet companies, and industry databases.
- Contact all database departments and confirm that your book is in their systems.

- Create packages containing sample chapters, a color cover, and a table of contents.
- Hire publicity and marketing firms or create publicity and marketing plans on your own.

FIVE MONTHS BEFORE YOUR BOOK'S PUB DATE:

- Send sales packets to the wholesale and retail buyers.
- Write cover copy and marketing plan for back of the Advance Reader's Copy.
- Design ARC.
- Send ARC files to digital printer.

FOUR MONTHS BEFORE YOUR BOOK'S PUB DATE:

- Send ARCs to buyers.
- Call buyers to follow up and present book information. Request promotion and placement for your book. (Do not be surprised if they tell you that they need to see the actual book before making a final decision. This is common and actually good news for you.)
- Research potential promotion and placement opportunities appropriate for your book (front-of-store tables, postcard mailings, Internet ads . . .).
- Check to see that all databases have your book information and have entered tit correctly.
- Send ARCs to reviewers.

THREE MONTHS BEFORE YOUR BOOK'S PUB DATE:

- Call reviewers to follow up on review packages.
- Buy ads and initiate marketing for launch during pub month.
- Follow up with store newsletters and online retailers and start writing guest articles to be published on their sites during your pub month.

TWO MONTHS BEFORE YOUR BOOK'S PUB DATE:

- Send finished books to buyers with request for orders and updates on your marketing buys. If they decline to order from a wholesaler, offer them the books on consignment.
- (Consignment is a program where you sell the book to the store at a 40 percent discount off of the retail price. They receive and stock the books but do not pay you until the books sell. It is your responsibility to check on the sales once a month and invoice based on sales reported.)
- Participate in a library outreach campaign through your distributor or find a service that allows publishers to announce books to librarians.
- Send copies of your finished book to companies, corporations, and catalogs that you feel best represent your book's audience.

ONE MONTH BEFORE YOUR BOOK'S PUB DATE:

- Call all key buyers and confirm orders are in place.

THE MONTH OF YOUR BOOK'S PUB DATE:

- Keep an eye on sales and stocking and ask buyers to reorder. They have too many books to keep track of yours.

PRESENTING YOUR BOOK

If you are a first-time publisher and wish to have your book considered by the major wholesalers and retailers in the U.S., here is a basic overview of who they are and how they work. These companies are not the entirety of the industry, but they do make up a very large percentage of your possible venues.

AMAZON.COM

There are a couple of different ways to get your book into Amazon.com.

If you have printed copies and want to sell them directly to Amazon yourself, use Amazon Advantage. When you have your books in a warehouse (or guest room), ready for orders, go to *www.amazon.com/advantage* and sign up. Amazon will give you an opportunity to post your book's information and cover. As orders come in to Amazon from your readers, Amazon will order the books from you. The orders are required to be at a 55 percent discount and on consignment. Monthly sales and payment reports are available online. As your sales increase, Amazon will order larger and larger stock up orders.

You can also choose to sell the books yourself as a third-party book seller. You sign up for Amazon Seller Central and create a store on Amazon. The books will not be eligible for Amazon Prime shipping or other marketing options, but keep most of the profits as you are the one selling the book, not Amazon. You are just using Amazon as a storefront. They take a small cut and you ship the books to the customer yourself.

If you have decided to go POD, CreateSpace will keep your book in stock and available to Prime members at all times.

BUT DON'T NEGLECT THE OTHER ONLINE RETAILERS!

If your book is on a brick and mortar bookstore website, you have a real shot of moving it to a test in the stores. Don't drive all of your online traffic to Amazon . . . make sure you have people buy from and review on the other bookstore sites too!

www.indiebound.org
www.bn.com
www.booksamillion.com
www.chapters.ca

Do You Need Amazon Advantage?
—By Carew Papritz, author of The Legacy Letters

I often hear clients struggle with the idea of signing up for Amazon Advantage. They wonder why they can't just list their book on Amazon as a third party seller. I wanted to share with you the experience of a client who decided to sign up for Advantage after I "pushed" a little.

I'm an independent publisher with an award-winning book that is being reviewed and sold nationally. I'm also an Amazon Central Seller. I make more profit because of their amazingly low fulfillment prices and access to an incredible book market. BUT, even though I have thousands of books in three different fulfillment centers, I'm still a "third-party" seller. I will NEVER get that most important little green "Buy Button" on Amazon because they still control all the little green "Buy Buttons" for BMVD—Books, Movies, Videos, and DVDs. (If you sold waffle makers or nail clippers, you'd get a "Buy Button.")

The only way to get that little "Buy Button" is through the Amazon Advantage program. I'll be honest. I don't like the Amazon Advantage program because it's a consignment program. BUT it's the only game in town that will get you the "Buy Button" for your book. The ONLY game in town.

That little "Buy Button" on Amazon means EVERYTHING to sell your book.

It means more than Amazon Author Central—more than even good reviews—more than everything. It means, in the eyes of the Amazon consumer, you are legit. I'm still an Amazon Central Seller and still have prices lower than Amazon. I'm still the only third-party seller with prime shipping rights. But I will never, ever, ever get that little green "Buy Button." And nor will you. And what's really sad is without that "Buy Button," you'll be dumped in and lumped in with all the third-party sellers, which doesn't give your book the appearance of Amazon legitimacy. That's the reality of Amazon.

I learned all this Amazon information the hard way. It's not written in bold anywhere. I am ALL for the independent author and publisher to make it. But there's the Amazon Advantage way—or the highway. And yes, I did, finally get that little green "Buy Button."

BOOK CHAINS

The two largest book chains in the U.S. are Barnes & Noble and Books-A-Million. If you are a publisher who would like to sell your books to Barnes & Noble or through BN.com, you must become a vendor of record with their warehouse.

Send a copy of your book, title information, marketing plan, and cover letter to:

Barnes & Noble, Inc.
Small Press Department
122 Fifth Avenue
New York, NY 10011

After three to four weeks, you will receive a response and an answer to your book's prospects at Barnes & Noble.

If you get a yes, the wholesaler will receive the order and you may not even know that B&N received the books. You will also not know WHICH stores received the books.

But once you know the books have shipped to B&N, go to *www.bn.com* and search for your book. You can type in a zip code and search for stores that have it in stock!

Books-A-Million, Inc., also has a new-vendor process. Send a copy of your book, sales sheet, marketing plan, and cover letter to:

Director of Merchandising
Booksamillion.com
P.O. Box 19728
Birmingham, AL 35219

It takes two to three months to get through the system there and hear back from their buying department about the decision made about stocking your title. This decision will come in the form of a letter.

This is your one chance to make a good first impression on Books-A-Million and Barnes & Noble. Do not hurry or rush your package. Be sure to provide them with a full accounting of your marketing plans, a copy of your press release, and a cover letter with a full explanation of why your book will be successful.

If the chains don't accept your book, do not be discouraged. Once you have developed a sales history from online sales and a fully executed marketing program, you can approach the chains again with your updated information. The key to successful book sales is not a great initial pitch to the chains but having the patience to make several great pitches over the first few months of a book's life. When you contact the buyers for an additional chance at being stocked on their shelves, make sure that you have a strong, new set of reasons why they should stock the book. If they said no to your original pitch, they will not say yes to your original pitch reworded.

If your book is taken in by a bookstore chain, your job is not over. Once a month (and only once a month), contact the buyer with updated marketing successes and ask for your sales and inventory numbers. Keep track of the sales and inventory and do not hesitate to ask the store to stock more copies of your book if your sales are strong.

What is a strong sale? The general rule of thumb is that if you sell approximately 10 percent of a store's inventory each week, you should ask for more stock on their shelves.

INDEPENDENT BOOKSTORES

While the state of the independent bookstore in America is in constant flux, there has been a recent improvement in the outlook for the local, neighborhood bookstore. In 2007, for the first time in nineteen years, more independent bookstores opened than closed. Consumers and local shoppers have started to return to the smaller, more personal stores for the local flavor and sense of community.

However, reaching and pitching your book to the more than 2,000 independent bookstores is very difficult and time consuming. Luckily, the American Booksellers Association has a number of marketing and promotional packages to help small publishers get their books in front of the buyers of these stores.

The majority of these stores prefer to buy from Baker & Taylor or Ingram. So be sure to sign up with a wholesaler before approaching the bookstores.

Library Sales
By Linda K. Murdoch, Bellwether Books

As an independent publisher, I realized libraries were an important venue to pursue. My logic was to start with one state at a time and pursue the smaller libraries not inundated with marketing material. In this way, Bellwether Books would hopefully stand out. Plus, it is always good to use the local angle, as it gives you a focus and a defined target market. I could also set the groundwork for marketing future publications. As with everything I seem to get into, I needed to know more. I made a few calls, got my friend Barbara Osgood-Hartness with Poncha Press involved, and here's what we uncovered.

COLLECTIONS DEVELOPMENT VS. AQUISITIONS LIBRARIAN
Become familiar with these two terms, because they are the "who" of library marketing. The larger libraries use the term

"collections/development" to describe the person who holds what is often the most coveted position in public libraries: making the buying decisions. For smaller libraries, the term "acquisitions" is used. Of the roughly 15,000 public libraries, about 17 percent (or 2,600, possibly the same 2,600 on PMAs list) have an annual budget of more than $25,000. That's about 3,000–4,800 $8 paperbacks a year and a lot fewer hardcovers, depending upon whether the library is getting a discount or not (more about this later). Compare that to the 50,000-plus books published each year, and you understand the dilemma faced by the acquisitions librarian.

Most, like Sybil Harrison, the collections/development manager for Jefferson County Public Library near Denver, take their positions seriously. They are public servants, since libraries receive their funding through tax dollars. The criteria, according to Ms. Harrison, appear simple. They have to consider what the people using their library want, as well as what they need. That often comes down to a well-written, well-presented book that fills a niche not already accommodated in their library; one that appeals to the regional public they serve.

They do want to hear recommendations for good books, from book reviewers, bloggers, distributors/wholesalers, readers, small press representatives, and even individual publishers. And some do feel responsible enough to look at all the material sent to them. They like to see a short synopsis of the book, with easy access to ordering information. ISBNs are a must.

They like to know the credentials of the author in order to feel confident that the information inside the book is reliable. What they don't want is for someone to send them a book, call them by phone, or solicit by e-mail. Take the "self" out of the term self-publisher and you will garner more respect. By the way, libraries buy materials all year round, although they may have more money at the start of the calendar year.

HOW TO MARKET TO LIBRARIES

There are a couple of key wholesalers and distributors that serve the library market. They offer discounts of 42 to 45 percent on hardbound books, 30 to 35 percent on paperbacks, and, depending upon the volume, free shipping. They even process the books by offering labels, barcodes, etc., for about $2 a book, which is cheaper than the libraries can process them with their limited staff. There are non-profit publishers, such as university presses, that give smaller discounts (about 10 percent).

So as an independent publisher, it's an uphill battle trying to compete with these major players. This is especially true when we are told to market to libraries because we don't have to discount as deeply. keep in mind that libraries are less likely to buy from a small-discounting publisher, especially if it means complicating (adding numerous vendors to) their accounting system. So why should they buy from you at full price plus shipping? It comes down to a business decision for both parties involved. For a library to buy your book at retail plus postage, it may mean giving up two equally desirable and more proven (publicized in *ALA Booklist, Library Journal,* etc.) books from the wholesaler. Selling your books to libraries at or near retail may mean positioning yourself out of the market.

Having said that, libraries will go directly to a publisher if they want your book in their collection and your book isn't available through a wholesaler/distributor. Some librarians mention that being able to purchase by credit card would keep their paperwork to a minimum. So to encourage direct purchases, perhaps offer a discount similar to that of distributors. (For postage, you can use library rates to mail to libraries, which is cheaper than the media rate.) By asking full price, we make ourselves less competitive.

LIBRARY READING GROUPS

More libraries find themselves in competition with the Internet, and need ways to attract patrons. One way is through reading groups. It might behoove you to ask librarians if they have reading groups that meet at the library and what topics/books are being discussed. Find out the group's specialty (mysteries, bestsellers, classic literature, etc.), or better yet, see if their reading picks are listed online. If your book fits into or complements this genre or title, offer to send them information about your book for their group. Include a few discussion questions to pique their curiosity. Make sure to include your business card (and contact information) with your website so they can buy your book.

HOW TO MARKET TO NON-PUBLIC LIBRARIES

Public libraries are only the tip of the iceberg. Let's say you have a book that is technically oriented. There are special business and research libraries that may be eager to get their hands on your book. Approaching businesses may even lead to the use of your book as a premium. Although technically oriented and usually restricted to staff use, you may have a topic that would appeal to hospital libraries. Don't be discouraged if only one book is ordered. It doesn't mean you've spent a lot of marketing time with little result. You never know what or who may turn that book into a bestseller.

Small town college libraries often dwarf that town's public library. If that school's learning resource center is open to the public, why not try placing your book there? Keep in mind that books will be chosen based on how they support the current curriculum. If you have a book on welding, community colleges or high schools with shop activities may be a market. If your book is on cooking techniques, as mine is, approach culinary schools or community colleges with cooking programs. Even high schools still teach what we used to call home economics. Sometimes the offshoot to all this are teachers who love your book and don't mind you quoting them. That gives you the credibility to approach others in the same field.

CORRECTIONAL FACILITIES

Many correctional facilities have both a law library and a general reading library. In New York, the state prison population is around 70,000, ranging in size from 250 to 3,000 inmates per facility. Although budgets have been tightened since September 2001, the inmates are starving for things to do and, if you'll excuse the pun, they are a captive audience. (Women's facilities receive many more donations than do men's, according to Jean Clancy Botta, who is on the library committee for the American Correctional Association.) Reading in prison makes sense. As Ms. Clancy Botta implied, reading helps to educate, and education has proven to decrease repeat offenses. Note that it is difficult to find books for prisoners, since many of them have such poor reading skills.

MUSEUMS AND SUBJECT-RELATED LIBRARIES

Historical museums have libraries that may want your book, especially if it depicts a subject related to their own location. For example, a book on mining may sell equally well in any mining community, whether in Colorado, California, or Alaska. If it includes photos of mining operations, that makes it even more attractive. For all of you who are writing your family history, historical/genealogical libraries are a great place to market, especially in the region(s) where your ancestors lived.

Have you written a book concerning a relative who was a Holocaust survivor? There are Jewish libraries that may be interested in that topic. Many religious libraries have books concerning moral issues, including philosophy, addiction, business ethics, etc.

I was surprised to find so many libraries that cater to the deaf and blind, both in public, private, and school libraries. Teaching facilities for these individuals would welcome large print, Braille, and audio books.

There are numerous government specialty libraries that can include anything from the National Park Service (environmental issues, botany, etc.) to the National Center for Atmospheric Research in Boulder, Colorado. Don't forget the military, where installations can have libraries on military history, aeronautics, etc.

Not only are there many kinds of libraries, including libraries just for librarians, but each has its own specialty. It's safe to say that if you wrote a book on the history of Wray, Colorado, the local public library, the nearest historical museum, or society, its surrounding counties, and even the larger city libraries in the same state may just want to buy a copy. Many of the libraries in your state will want history books about their state, its industry, its pioneers, and its way of life. For Colorado, the hot topic is southwestern history. Who knows, the local paper (which often has a library of its past newspaper publications) might do a large spread on your book about their hometown and then everyone may want a copy!

Shocking as this may sound, consider donating your book to libraries with less funding. Don't be shy about asking the local librarian to display your book as a way of announcing it to their community. I would venture to say that your potential for sales (from your order form in the back of the book) is as good, if not better than, your sales potential from newspaper reviews, for which you must also provide a free book.

So if you are focusing on libraries, focus your energies on your home turf first. Then if you can tear yourself away from the Internet, get to know the libraries in your state.

► Linda K. Murdock is the author and publisher of three books, *A Busy Cook's Guide to Spices, Almost Native: How to Pass as a Coloradan,* and *Mystery Lover's Puzzle Book.* All are available at www.bellwetherbooks.com.

WAL-MART, COSTCO AND AIRPORTS

When I meet authors and publishers who are interested in growing their sales, I ask them this question: "What shelves to you want to see your book sitting on?"

What I hear the most often is "Costco", "Wal-Mart" and often, "My book would be PERFECT for Airport stores!" While that may be true, I hate having to tell them what I am about to tell you . . .

"Your book will only get into a large chain store if you have already sold enough copies elsewhere to prove to the buyers at these stores that your book will be worth their time and shelf space."

Airport stores, Costco and Supermarkets have very limited shelf space compared to the rent they are being charged. It is a book buyer's job to make sure that those shelves earn their keep. Each inch of shelf space needs to yield a minimum amount of money each month. If books are put on the shelves that don't sell enough, the buyer has to replace them. This is expensive and a waste of time and money for the store.

So buyers are judged by how well they choose books that will sell well and make money per shelf spot. The best buyers have an innate sense of the books that will succeed. All buyers (if they are smart) look at data and sales history to back up their gut feelings before they put a book on their shelves.

No matter how great your book is, a buyer needs to PROVE to their companies that a book will make money. You need to prove to the buyer that your book will make money. How will you do that?

Airport stores don't have the luxury of trying out books to "see how they do." They choose books that have already done well in the book market or online.

One buyer I work with needs to make $3,000 off of every title on her shelves each month. Does your book sell $3,000 worth of units each month?

Sales reps pitching books to Wal-Mart from major publishing houses KNOW not to present ANY book that is not scheduled to sell over 10,000 copies in the first year. Minimum. That is the BARE MINIMUM. This is because Wal-Mart needs to know that the book, given a few inches of their very valuable shelf space, has already proven that it will "earn its keep."

So, before you approach the national offices of any of the major chains, you HAVE to have data that shows that they will make the money they are required to make. If you don't have sales from Amazon or the book retail chains, then you can try approaching a manager of a local airport store or Costco and ask if you can do an event. A successful book sales day at Costco can be leveraged into a conversation with the main buyer in Washington.

I am not saying that you cannot have your book accepted into Target . . . I am just letting you know what the book buyer's job looks like and what you will be up against.

Resources

For a list of current resources, updated
every week, please visit:
www.newshelves.com/resources

Glossary Of Terms

Advanced Reader's Copy (ARC) A prepublication copy of a book released before the final printing. A publisher will send ARCs out for marketing and publicity purposes to generate interest in the book.

Agent A professional within the book industry who represents an author and the author's work to publishers.

Back Matter Printed material that follows the main text of a book. Back matter may include, but is not limited to, an appendix, afterword, and index.

Backlist A list of a publisher's titles that are still in print but not recently published.

Bleed Printing to the very edge of the paper. Often the paper is cut to ensure that the print does not stop short of the edge.

Books in Print (BIP) A comprehensive resource for libraries, bookstores, and publishers, produced by R.R. Bowker.

Buyer A person or group of people responsible for choosing and purchasing the books that a retailer will sell to the public.

Chain A large corporation that owns several bookstores under one name.

CMYK A color model used in commercial printing that creates all colors by using a combination of cyan, magenta, yellow, and black.

Co-op A co-operative. Advertising produced by a bookseller, the cost of which is shared by the publisher.

Copy Editor A professional within the book industry who edits a manuscript for grammar, spelling, word usage, style, and clarity of writing.

Copy Editing A form of editing that focuses on grammar, spelling, word usage, style, and clarity of writing.

Design The arrangement of text, illustrations, page numbers, running heads, margins, front matter and back matter, as well as the designation of fonts and graphics, to create a book's layout.

Digital Printing A printing technology that is able to print a book directly from a computer file.

Distribution The process of moving books into the retail market.

Distributor A company a publisher hires to handle the sales, warehousing, shipping, and billing of its books.

DPI Dots per inch. DPI refers to the degree of resolution determined by the number of dots printed per linear inch. The higher the DPI, the greater the resolution and quality.

EAN Bar Code The translation of an ISBN into barcode form for electronic scanning.

Editor A professional within the book industry who evaluates a manuscript as a whole and edits the manuscript for organization, tone, consistency, clarity, flow, and logic. The editor will rework or rewrite the text as necessary and offer suggestions to the author, requesting that he or she flesh out an idea, clarify an issue, and/or resolve faulty logic. Sometimes called a developmental editor, structural editor, substantive editor, or content editor.

Folio Page number.

Font A complete set of characters available in a specific size and style of typeface.

Font Embedding The process of installing a font within a document to ensure that the font is available for that document even if the receiving computer does not have that particular font.

Front Matter Printed material that precedes the main text of a book. Front matter may include, but is not limited to, a title page, copyright page, table of contents, dedication, and introduction.

Frontlist A list of a publisher's new titles that are being released in the current season.

Fulfillment The activities involved in processing an order, including invoicing, accounts receivable, collections, shipping and handling, warehousing, and maintaining customer, sales, and inventory records.

Galley An unbound typeset copy of a book for review and/or proofreading.

Genre A specific category of literature. Examples of genres include romance, science fiction, mystery, true crime, etc.

Gutter The white space of the inner margins where two pages come together in a two-page spread.

Halftones The reproduction of an image using tiny dots to create gradations of light.

ISBN International Standard Book Number. A series of thirteen digits specific to the book industry that identifies the group or country of the publication, publisher, and title.

Layout The overall design of a book.

Margins The white space around the main body of text on a page.

Marketing A process of advertising and promoting an author's work.

Midlist The books in a publisher's catalogue that still sell quite well in spite of not being new. Perennial bestsellers.

Offset Printing A high-quality printing technique in which an image is transferred from a plate to a rubber cylinder and then onto paper.

PDF Portable document format. An electronic document format that allows for the distribution of a digital file that maintains all the elements of the original. Developed by Adobe.

Pixel The smallest unit of an image.

POD Print On Demand. A business model using digital printing technology that allows books to be printed in small quantities, even one at a time, permitting publishers to print books as they are ordered.

Positioning Statement A 100-word statement that outlines for a potential buyer the reasons why a book will be of interest to their clients. This statement exists to talk about the potential market for a book and how the publisher plans to reach that market.

Press Release A written announcement of a book and/or author sent to the media in hopes of creating publicity.

Print Date The date that a book comes off the press and is shipped to the publisher.

Print Run The number of copies printed for a publisher at one time.

Proofreader A professional within the book industry who checks a typeset book for errors in text and design and makes corrections as necessary.

Proofreading The process of checking a typeset book for errors in text and design. Often, proofreading involves checking the typeset book against the copy edited manuscript to ensure that all changes have been incorporated into the final set.

Pub Date The official date a book is available for ordering or purchasing by the general public.

Publicity Media exposure of a book.

Recto Right-hand page.

Release Date The date a book is available for ordering by the wholesalers and retailers.

Remainders Overstocked or unsold copies of a book that are sold at a deep discount.

Resolution The clarity and quality of an image, measured in DPI.

Returns Unsold copies of a book returned to a publisher for a full refund.

Review Copy Free copy of a book sent by a publisher to obtain a review.

RGB A color model used in display screens that creates colors using a combination of red, green, and blue pixels.

Sales Kit A package of informative material used to persuade buyers to purchase a book. A sales kit includes, but is not limited to, a cover, a complete outline of the book, positioning and marketing statements, a few sample chapters, and a one-page sheet listing all the book's pertinent information.

Sans Serif A typeface that does not have lines finishing off the tops and bottoms of the strokes of letters.

Self-publishing The publishing of a work by the work's author.

Serif A typeface that has lines finishing off the tops and bottoms of the strokes of letters.

Ship Date The date that a publisher ships a title to its customers to fill waiting orders.

Table of Contents A list of the divisions of a book with corresponding page numbers. Divisions may include chapter numbers, chapter titles, part numbers, part titles, and/or section/subhead titles.

Target Audience The intended readers of a book. A target audience is a specific group defined by characteristics such as demographic, age, gender, lifestyle, etc.

Title Information Sheet A part of a sales kit that includes a book's pertinent information. A title information sheet includes: ISBN, title, subtitle, author's name, author's bio, author's hometown, 100-word description of book, order contact information, book category, retail price, page count, trim size, ship date, publication date, format, print run, co-op and advertising budget, title and ISBN of previous books by author or in the series, title and ISBN of books similar to featured book.

Trim Size The dimensions of a finished book.

TrueType Font A scalable font that will remain true to form when printed or displayed in any size. Developed by Apple.

Verso Left-hand page.

Warehousing The process of storing and stocking an inventory of books.

Wholesaler A company that buys books at a deep discount and warehouses them for orders from bookstores, libraries, and online retailers.

Amy Collins

THE MOST UP-TO-DATE, ENTERTAINING, & KNOWLEDGABLE

PUBLISHING INDUSTRY SPEAKER

FUNNY, SHARP, AND SMART

Amy Collins packs every speech with tons of industry tips and executable advice. She has been a Book Buyer for a chain of bookstores as well as a Sales Director for a large books and magazine publisher. Over the years, she has sold to Barnes & Noble, Target, Costco, Airport Stores, Books-A-Million, Wal-Mart, and other major chains. She helped launch several hugely successful private label publishing programs for Borders, PetSmart and CVS. In 2006, Amy started New Shelves Books, one of the fastest-growing book distribution, sales and marketing companies in North America.

Amy Collins is the author of *THE WRITE WAY: Everything You Need to Know About Publishing, Selling, and Marketing your Book.* A full, step-by-step plan to publish your books and eBooks and how make a profit!

Contact:

20 Office Parkway #126, Pittsford, NY 14534
518.261.1300 X301 | amy@newshelves.com
www.newshelvesdistribution.com